Ask Me Why I'm Not In Church

A Call for the Church to Get
Out of the Building

AN ANDERSON and CANTY PRODUCTION

WESTBOW
PRESS®
A DIVISION OF THOMAS NELSON
& ZONDERVAN

WestBow Press books may be ordered through booksellers or by contacting:

WestBow Press
A Division of Thomas Nelson & Zondervan
1663 Liberty Drive
Bloomington, IN 47403
www.westbowpress.com
1 (866) 928-1240

Unless otherwise noted, scripture quotations are taken from the Holy Bible, New International Version®, NIV®. Copyright © 1973, 1978, 1984, 2011 by Biblica, Inc.™ Used by permission of Zondervan. All rights reserved worldwide. www.zondervan.com The "NIV" and "New International Version" are trademarks registered in the United States Patent and Trademark Office by Biblica, Inc.™

Scripture quotations marked MSG are taken from THE MESSAGE, copyright © 1993, 2002, 2018 by Eugene H. Peterson. Used by permission of NavPress. All rights reserved. Represented by Tyndale House Publishers, Inc.

Scripture quotations marked KJV taken from the King James Version of the Bible.

ISBN: 978-1-9736-6471-0 (sc)
ISBN: 978-1-9736-6472-7 (hc)
ISBN: 978-1-9736-6470-3 (e)

Library of Congress Control Number: 2019906479

Print information available on the last page.

WestBow Press rev. date: 6/21/2019

<u>**Ask Me Why Endorsements**</u>

Anderson and Canty aren't providing three easy steps so you can clone their urban ministry model, nor are they doing armchair theology. Instead, Ask Me Why I'm Not In Church is overflowing with nuggets of wisdom from actual pastors leading a missional church in Philadelphia. Read this book with care as you live the Gospel in your neighborhood!

Drew Hart, PhD, Assistant Professor of Theology at Messiah College, author of *Trouble I've Seen: Changing the Way the Church Views Racism*

Dr. Anderson and Dr. Canty are highly experienced pastors who understand both how important it is to preach the gospel and how imperative it is to understand one's context. They also practice what they preach. In "Ask Me Why I'm Not in Church," they take the reader on a journey that begins with a stirring of the heart and ends with a missional community of faith. At times prophetic, at times devotional, "Ask Me Why I'm Not in Church" tackles any number of burning cultural issues and seeks to address them through the lens of the Bible. This is an ideal book for pastors, small groups, and Sunday school classes to read and discuss in order to learn how to better understand and reach the community around them. As Anderson and Canty note, our culture is changing rapidly, and this is a book that is sensitive to the needs of our culture yet also faithful in its preaching. This is a resource packed with personal stories, biblical teachings, practical applications, missional strategies (especially T4T), discussion questions, and just the right amount of theological insight. It will be a great addition to your church's ministry toolkit.

Derek Cooper, PhD, Associate Professor of World Christian History at Missio Seminary, author of *Christianity and World Religions: An Introduction to the World's Major Faiths*

Ask Me Why I'm Not in Church is a well-written book on how a church can become missional in context. Although it is largely formed around an extended case study of Great Commission Church in Philadelphia, PA, the book brings out many solid principles that can be applicable for all churches regardless of their context. Especially helpful is chapter 3 where the authors have selected Scripture passages that are familiar to most churchgoers and have made novel applications that can bring Scripture to life in 21ˢᵗ century church conversions to being missional. Churches in the U.S. seem to have lost their missional response to Scripture, and this is a must read for all those wrestling with God's Great Commission. This book is for church leaders/teachers who want to see their church move from being pew-centered to being missional within their unique community.

Susan Baker, PhD, Assistant Director of the Doctor of Ministry Program at Missio Seminary, author of *Understanding Mainland Puerto Rican Poverty*

The very useful and practical training in chapter 4 was excellent. And in chapter 3, you stress the various justice issues that are inherent in the community and the need for the church (or the seminary) to engage those issues. I fully support this missional approach at GCC. I was deeply encouraged to read about the incarnational ministry of your congregation. What struck me most was that I think much of what you did with GCC is applicable to MISSIO as we move to the city.

Frank James, PhD, President of Missio Seminary, co-author of, *Church History: Pre-Reformation to the Present, vol. 2*

This book is one of those rare gems that merges academically informed theology with practical ministry, leadership, pastoral, and real-life experience. The Anderson-Canty partnership seems to be something fashioned by the Spirit of God for achieving Kingdom goals, first in ground-level ministry, but now in merging their insights together to produce an extremely useful manual for fellow missional leaders. What brings you to this book? "I've always wondered if "missional" is just a buzzword. I mean, what is the big deal, theologically speaking?" You'll find the answer here. "I like how missional theology' captures some key biblical themes of Trinitarian theology; but what practical difference does it make on the ground?" You'll find the answer here. "Yes, I appreciate the ideals that 'missional ministry' embraces, but does anybody understand how difficult it is to actually try to lead real transition in a real church composed of real people?" Again—you'll find what you're looking for here!

R. Todd Mangum, PhD Clemens Professor of Missional Theology, Missio Seminary, author of *The Dispensational-Covenantal Rift*

Ask Me Why I'm Not In Church is a love letter to communities facing challenges, an instructional manual for street-level evangelism, and a frank and honest portrayal of one church's journey into the places where the saving message of Jesus Christ is still turning lives around. I believe this book will have a tremendous impact for Christ as other churches use it as a roadmap for evangelism.

Solomon Jones, author, Praise 107.9 radio host, and Philadelphia Daily News columnist

Dr. Larry Anderson and Dr. Kyle Canty have written a compelling account of the journey on which they led their church from the comfort of the suburbs of Philadelphia into the city to fulfill the mandate of Christ to "go into all the world and preach the Gospel." When many churches leave cities to escape violence and other conditions, they faced into the storm to bring the light and hope of Christ to those walking in darkness. Their bold journey has yielded much fruit because of their determination to take part in the mission of God. We need go no further than their introduction to feel Holy Spirit conviction for our " ...presuppositions and procrastination," while we "...[claim] "to love God all the while ignoring His mission." May God use the words in this well-written, well-documented book to ignite a fire in our souls to make God's mission our top priority.

Anthony W. Hurst, Sr. DMin, Associate Pastor, Church of God Adjunct Professor, Cairn and Eastern Universities

CONTENTS

Tables:

Acknowledgements

We want to thank the following institutions for providing world-class education and the tools that allowed us to engage in this kind of ministry. Thank you Missio Seminary for a cutting edge education in missional theology. Thank you Cairn University for a foundation in the sacred Scriptures. Thank you Baptist Resource Network for the opportunity to put into practice what we know and love. Thank you NAMB for the opportunity to reach the great city of Philadelphia and oversee the planting and flourishing of churches. We want to thank our readers Sue Baker, Derek Cooper, Solomon Jones, Al Tizon, Todd Mangum, David Lamb, Frank James, Andrew Hart, Shannon Baker, Pam Canty, and Barry Whitworth for the feedback you gave on the manuscript. You helped us shape it into becoming *Ask Me Why I'm Not In Church*, the book. We would like to thank our dear friend Anthony Hurst for being our first reader and editor; your contributions have been priceless. We also thank Shana Murph for being our second and final editor. We would also like to thank Manny Ortiz, who has gone home to be with the Lord, and Susan Baker for making time to mentor and guide the both of us. There have been too many others to name that have contributed to this work and for that we are eternally grateful.

Dr. Larry Anderson

First, I want to give glory to God. Hallelujah! Now, there are many people I would like to thank that helped us pen this book. I want to thank my wife Kim. You have been my sounding board and my ride or die partner from the corner to the cross. You've always believed in me and supported my dreams. My children, Marquis, Darius and Gabrielle, thank you for sacrificing some of your quality time so that I can not only write this book but live out the experiences which led to its penning. Thank you to Bill and Dollie Parker for embracing me, not as a son in law but as a son, and your enormous support. Thank you to Uncle David, AKA Bishop Hill for spiritually raising me up to accept my call. Thank you to my sister Lisa King and my brother Aaron Bryant for always being the close knit and supportive siblings Mom would have been so proud of. Thank you Great Commission Church, who for 15 years, has allowed me to grow and pastor you into the mission of God, which has been non-traditional, challenging and very rewarding—to God be the glory. And finally, I would like to thank our pastor, Hal J. Hopkins for challenging me from the very beginning of my ministry journey to embrace my own authenticity and enjoy the ride the Lord would take me on.

Dr. D. Kyle Canty

It is an exciting feeling to be able to thank those who came alongside us to complete this book. My wife Pam is usually the first person to hear some of my ideas and to provide a helpful critique of my thoughts. I am blessed to have her. She has taught me so much about writing. I am grateful for my children, Micah, Karis and Shiloh who give me so much hope for the generation to come. They are funny, brilliant and creative and a gift from God. I want to also thank my dad who helped me fall in love with Jesus and His mission early on in life. Thanks mom for always being in my corner no matter who or what. I learned so much about faithful living and sacrifice for the cause of Christ from my parents. I am also grateful to my parents by marriage and their love and acceptance of me as a son. Thank you Hal Hopkins for your pastor's heart. I thank Great Commission Church for the opportunity to serve and to be creative. We've been rocking together for 18 years and I have grown and learned so much.

INTRODUCTION

As the Director of Evangelism for Pennsylvania and South Jersey (Larry), and the NAMB Send City Coordinator for Philadelphia (Kyle), the two of us are constantly challenged with helping existing churches and church plants discover ways to equip the saints to engage the lost. In addition to our Bible college and seminary education, and the fact that we are both avid readers, we are blessed to serve together as pastors of a church in the city of Philadelphia. This gives us access to practice what we've learned firsthand serving the bride of Christ, the church, so we can be more than theorists or academics speculating on what may work. This book is filled with ways to help any church in any area push back darkness. It challenges the presuppositions and procrastination of people claiming to love God all the while ignoring His Mission.

In North America church attendance is down, authentic conversions are down, baptisms are down, yet the church still continues to operate like it's business as usual. We understand how, post Christendom, the church is being systematically and culturally marginalized, but we don't understand how we can participate in marginalizing ourselves. The world says the Bible is archaic, our God is intolerant and church people are hypocrites, yet we do nothing to challenge these perceptions. Of course, when I say we do nothing, I'm exaggerating. However, it's the church's lack of commitment to getting out of the four walls of the building, which has ignited the fire behind the penning of this book. That's what *Ask Me Why I'm Not In Church* is all about. It's about getting the church (the people of God) out of the buildings of God to participate in the mission of God, which is redeeming the lost.

Remember when you got saved and the scales fell from your eyes? Remember when you came to know without a shadow of a doubt that God was real? Remember when you came to realize that Jesus Christ was truly the visible image of the invisible God? Remember when you realized all of your past sins and even your present and future ones would no longer be counted against you? Remember how amazing of a day that was? Your rescue mission was better than anything Marvel, or DC Comics could have ever come up with. And after you got saved and blessed with eternal life, you were then instructed to get baptized, join the church, and fall in line with the other survivors who were once as excited as you were.

So the extinguishing of the fire routine begins. The excitement of the church says we got another new worker and potential tither, in contrast to the excitement of the new believer whose fire is begging to be a part of a rescue team to be trained to go out and save the world. As Iron Man told the young Peter Parker, *stay in your lane bro, you're not ready to save the world!* My paraphrasing of course. The church tells the young believer, "Be in the world not of the world, and stay away from your unbelieving friends and family; they'll only cause you to fall back into that sinful world."

If we were to fast forward our superhero Christian movie and check back in on our excited new believer, it would be hard to find him now because he's becoming so polished and starting to look and sound just like the other survivors. He is now singing on the choir, attending a small group and enjoying the Sunday sermon. He has settled in and he's becoming a really good "churchian." However, every once in a while the urge to break out of the walls of the church arises and the passion to take a rescue mission out to the world to save the lost ascends, but then he reminds himself: the church has a friends and family day where they invite those out there to come in here, and so he goes back to business as usual. Fade to black ...

What is a really good "churchian?" Glad you asked. It's what we become when we spend all of our time, talent and treasure in the building we call the church. It's when our spiritual life is disconnected from mostly all other aspects of our life. Where do I talk about God? Church. Where do I worship God? Church. Where do I serve God? Church. Where do I go to hear from God? Church. The Greek word for church, ekklesia, means the called out /assembly, referring to a group of people separated from darkness and gathering together around the Light. That Light is the Lord Himself, who rescued us and blessed us to become His sons and daughters. How interesting is it that some people so clearly see the church as a building while others see it as a body of believers?

To follow in the footsteps of our Brother Jesus Christ to become Christians, the suffix *ian* means of the same property or character of, or better yet a follower of. So we are called to be followers of Christ, and that means we do what we have seen and heard from Christ. Simple enough right? Well, two quick questions: When you read the Gospel accounts of Jesus' life, how much time do you see Him spending in the temple, synagogue or what we might call the church? Now read the Gospels again and tell me how much time do you see Jesus spending amongst the people? The comparison of time between the community and the church is not even close. But why? It's not because Jesus did not value the temple; it's not because He was anti church; it's because He came to seek and save the lost. It was not the righteous He was after but the unrighteous. And although it's obvious there were surely some lost and unrighteous folks in the temple, the world, which He would die for, was where He spent the bulk of His time.

"Ask Me Why I'm Not In Church" is a slogan we coined and put on T-shirts to send our people out in the community to love on the lost. On Sunday mornings they would adopt locations within the community filled with people who did not have attending church on their radar. They would hang in a laundromat and give out quarters to people to help them wash or dry their clothes. They would adopt a corner known for prostitution and offer prayer to the young ladies of the night. Undoubtedly, the provocative shirts our members would wear would draw the curiosity of an onlooker to ask them why they were not in church. The person would expect to hear something negative about the church and think that our people were in rebellion or worse a cult. However, our members would share some wonderful responses that communicated they were the church and there's no way they could be doing what they were doing if they only stayed in the building.

Ask Me Why I'm Not in Church is a book we decided to write for pastors, evangelism leaders, and lay people who feel called to motivate their church, their team or their small group to get out of the building and into the community to start making a real impact in the lives of their neighbors. There is a famous saying that asks the question: If your church was to move out of the community, would anyone care? If you can honestly answer that question in the negative, then this book is for you. If you don't know the names of the neighbors surrounding your church, then this book is for you. If you don't know the needs, the struggles, the history and the trajectory of your community, then this book is for you.

Our desire is to share our story, to share some resources and insights to help you and your church. It's not a "read and duplicate what we did" book. But it's a "you're not alone book" and "have you ever thought about this?" kind of book. It's also not a church growth book. Although, if you begin to impact your community in some real transformative ways, numerical and spiritual growth will be a byproduct. The goal is to reignite the fire in church. The goal is to prepare Christian superheroes to go out into the world and participate in the greatest rescue mission ever orchestrated. In John 20:21 Jesus said, "As the Father has sent me, I am sending you" NIV. We are the sent ones. Each of us, should we choose to accept it, has been uniquely called and gifted for a mission. We have individually and collectively been placed in a context that requires our services. We must pick up our mats and walk; we must share the Good News of our own rescue and offer the same opportunity to others.

In chapter 1 I, Larry, share the story of our church, which moved from the suburbs of Philadelphia, PA back into the heart of the city. This move was filled with many challenges as you will see but it was one that could only take place when we all submitted to the mission of God. Chapter 2 is meant to help you biblically move those who are following you in the right direction. It deals with many of the excuses we have encountered in training other churches to become Kingdom and mission focused. We believe the best way to get someone one to follow God's plan is to use God's Word. Therefore, these brief Bible lessons are designed to equip you and encourage you to add on to these lessons by really seeing God's Word as an instructional manual. Chapter 3 was written to teach you how to navigate some of the toughest issues facing our church bodies today.

We must always remember the world we are deploying our members into. We must understand the non-biblical voices, influences and positions they are subjected to 24-7. The music, movies and muckety-mucks who have their ears on a daily basis. These mini Bible lessons were given to help give you and your congregation a Biblical worldview. Our hope is that this chapter would motivate you to develop a robust toolbox that helps a believer to intelligently stand on his own beliefs with sound doctrine to support them. Chapters 4 through 6 share the training needed for a congregation or a small group and some lessons learned from a church that actually did it.

After 10 years of being in the city of Philadelphia, ministry is as exciting as ever. The fire is burning ever so brightly. All new believers that have been rescued, is told from the moment they come in that they are now being trained to go back out. They understand the church is not the ending place but the sending place. As you read this book, we are praying for revitalization in your church. We are praying that what you read in these pages will confirm for you that the mission of God is alive and well and you have a place in it. But like a great meal, this book is meant to be shared. Don't read this in isolation; challenge others to join you in this walk. I, Larry, always told my students in seminary that if they read in isolation, they can and will grow in isolation. And the worse thing about growing in isolation is the frustration that others are just not on the same page. So, don't let that be you. God is up to something and you grabbing this book is just the beginning.

We pray that you are 1) encouraged as you read about our church's journey from a middle-class suburb to the city of Philadelphia. 2) edified as you wrestle with the exegesis of passages that have been specifically chosen to address hot button cultural issues. 3) able to evaluate the excuses of the church in relation to your own posture or to challenge others who may reflect them. 4) equipped to exegete your church and your community to develop a strategy to connect the two and 5) become enthusiastic about the results you see and the possibilities your church could experience.

-Dr. Larry Anderson and Dr. Kyle Canty

CHAPTER 1

Suburbs To City

In this chapter I, Larry, highlight the beginning of our ministry. Before we started ministering abroad and helping others move outside of their comfort zone, God moved us out of our own. This chapter gives you a glance at the pain, prayer, process, preaching, preparation and progression that Great Commission Church (GCC) and we as pastors went through to move from the suburbs into the city to follow the mission of God.

The Pain

The year was 2007, and the skyrocketing murder rate of young black men in Philadelphia was overwhelmingly tragic. As the race for mayor was underway, every day the media would publicize the death toll. The tragic senseless killings rose and over time the victims were being callously identified by numbers and not by their names. I thought to myself, how could the media be so insensitive? On one occasion, I went to buy the *Philadelphia Daily News* at my local Wawa mini market, and within earshot I could hear a question that underscored the dismissive perspective of many outside of communities impacted by these murders. "What number are we at now?" As shocking as it might sound to others, to those within this store it was voiced in the same tone used to describe the mid-season record for the Eagles or Sixers. The number they were referring to was not a score to be heartlessly discussed, but a life taken by violence.

Then I reflected on the fact that the majority of the people doing the killing look like me and the majority of the people getting killed look like me. Almost every night I would hear on the news that a young man was murdered in North Philadelphia. But this was not the North Philly I remembered growing up in. I had great memories of playing basketball on the street with a milk crate nailed to a light pole, racing popsicle sticks down the street using water from the fire hydrant, cutting a tennis ball in half and using a broom stick to play a game of baseball, which we called "Halfies," and filling bottle tops with tar to play a game called "Deadman." Did people get killed back then? Yes, but they were real enemies and there was real beef, not because you were accused of looking at someone wrong, stepping on their toe, or wearing the wrong color, or any other menial thing that caused a conflict.

The church during those days was a part of the community. The people in the neighborhood knew the pastor of the local church even if they did not attend. I remember our local pastor would walk the streets and introduce himself to different people and let them know about vacation bible school, free cheese giveaway day or something that the community could come and join in on. I also remember how when people would get into trouble with the law, they would always go to the pastor for a character reference or have him with them when they turned themselves in. The pastor was trusted; he was a peacemaker and a strong pillar in the community.

We fast forward the clock to 2007, and oh how my heart ached and how I remember feeling overwhelmed and helpless. The natural connections from the church to the community, which existed in the past, seemed to be missing. The pastor who was once a known role model and one of the most respected people in any community, was now virtually unknown and seen as an opportunist, a relic or worse. And so I wondered how could I, just one pastor of one small church make a difference when we as a community and a city were facing such a huge problem?

The Prayer

With this fatalistic backdrop of the city, I'm pastoring a church in Abington, PA and wondering what I can possibly do about this. I'm praying and asking God if it is time for me to leave my church and start something new in Philadelphia. I identified with Luke 19:41,42 and Jesus weeping over Jerusalem knowing what would bring them peace, yet also knowing He would be rejected. I knew I would not be able to do a whole lot by myself so I prayed God would partner me with someone in the Kingdom whose heart was breaking like mine. The Lord did not instantly give me a clear answer so I assembled the men from the church and made an invitation to men in the community to come and join a study of the book of Nehemiah to see what the Lord would have us to do in response to these tragic conditions.

The study of Nehemiah ignited a fire in the men from our church. They likened the rebuilding of the burned down "walls" of Jerusalem to repairing the brokenness of urban families in Philadelphia. God began to illuminate the text to help our observations. Our investigation determined that absentee fathers, teenage pregnancy, drug addicted parents, easy access to firearms, and the lack of godly role models were just some of the issues perpetuating this tragic condition. The Lord spoke to us through these prayers and challenged us to go into the city and partner with other churches in prayer to get even more saints prepared for battle. And so the process began.

The Process

GCC began participating in prayer walks with other churches in Philadelphia. These walks would be in some pretty dangerous areas. In those moments we discovered the truth of the Scripture that taught us to "watch and pray." As cars sped by, loud music and profanity rang out at random, and I could see the uneasiness in our men. As time went on, we developed a system where some of us would watch and the others would pray and the rotation would continue. Shout out to Pastor Clarence Hester from Erie Ave Baptist Church for allowing us to tag along.

We also joined a group of city churches that were participating in gun buy backs in the neighborhood playgrounds. My friend Pastor Kevin Aiken, from Heart of Worship, the chief organizer, would have a stage prepared and several of us gospel-driven conscientious preachers would preach a sermonette of peace and hope to those in attendance. You would literally have people walking pass you with guns in their hands, asking you where they could get their food voucher for turning in their unwanted firearms.

These event-oriented ministry endeavors were successful projects, but they seemed to have no lasting effects, which we could monitor. In addition, after each of these events, my church would return to our suburban location and wonder what was next. It was this spiritual struggle that left me unsettled until the next event. The wrestling match between my heart in Philadelphia and my body and church body being in the suburbs of Philadelphia became overwhelming. Finally, I felt led to share with the congregation my personal struggles of remaining at Great Commission Church as a pastor in the suburbs. Their response to me was one that still amazes me, and it affirmed the Lord's hand in all we were doing. The church body responded that they mirrored my passion and desire to have a greater presence and process to address the tragedies taking place in the city. In addition, they communicated they were interested in doing whatever I believed God was calling us to do in response to this.

Now it was not just the Nehemiah Bible study that had prepared them for this moment. My preaching was based in a missional hermeneutic that would not allow me to separate proclamation from demonstration. In other words, a holistic gospel that ministered to the felt and spiritual needs was what I had been proclaiming since I became the pastor. I would often read Jesus quoting Isaiah in Luke 4:18,19, "The Spirit of the Lord is on me, because he has anointed me to preach good news to the poor. He has sent me to proclaim freedom for the prisoners and recovery of sight for the blind, to release the oppressed, to proclaim the year of the Lord's favor" (NIV). I would invite the congregation to wrestle with James' challenge in James 2:17 of faith without works being dead. I asked could we tell a brother or sister without clothes or food to "Go, I wish you well, keep warm and well fed?" So it was the Holy Spirit moving hearts through the Word that touched this middle class suburban church to care deeply for the inner city.

The Preaching

While many preachers will mock seminary training as if it does not prepare you for the real world, I must applaud the teaching I received from Biblical Theological Seminary (now Missio Seminary) for their pioneering work in Missional Theology. Preaching the Bible with a missional hermeneutic was the catalyst that moved our congregation to see the *missio dei*, or the mission of God, as the true calling of the church. This brief preaching bullet point is critical for preachers and teachers but might seem a little academic for the lay person, but please understand it's critical if you are leading others.

God's missional nature demands an active pursuit of man by God for redemption. Therefore, a missional hermeneutic provides a lens that gives us the ability to track the activity of the Israelites as God's chosen nation throughout the Old Testament, as well as observe the church's activity on earth after the day of Pentecost. A missional hermeneutic is employed to discover how God has sought to reconcile the world to himself with the truth of his Gospel since the beginning of time. In other words, "A missional hermeneutic proceeds from the assumption that the whole Bible renders to us the story of God's mission through God's people in their engagement with God's world for the sake of the whole of God's creation."[1]

The passage traditionally entitled "the Great Commission," regarded as the last words of Jesus to his disciples in Matthew 28:19, begins with the words, "Therefore go and make disciples of all nations ." (NIV) The word "go" (poreuomai) is a verb defined at times as walk or depart, and carries with it a command to carry on. This word "go" is a transfer of responsibility, and ultimately the pursuit of a journey. These words of Jesus are a commission to actively pursue the discipleship of all mankind in order for them to come to a saving knowledge of Christ himself. A healthy understanding

---

[1] Wright, C. J. (2010). *The mission of God's people: A biblical theology of the churches mission*. Grand Rapids, MI: Zondervan.51

5

of God's mission will oppose the stagnant posture of a church fixated on simply inviting attendees to come. A missional hermeneutic understands that the word "go" is a marching order, which unleashes the soldiers of Christ, equipped with the full armor of God, to embark on a mission to redeem the world. As with any mission, the culture, context, and citizens must be studied in order to sustain a healthy pursuit.

Great Commission Church understood it could not fulfill the call of God to go and make disciples if it did not exit its church doors and venture into the community seeking to save the lost. "The Spirit calls, guides, and empowers the community of Christ's followers, the Church, as the socially, historically, and culturally embodied witnesses to the gospel of Jesus Christ and the tangible expression of the mission of God"[2] It is evident that God's presence is made known to man through the proclamation of his Word (Romans 10:14) and the demonstration of his love (Luke 10:35-37). A missional hermeneutic will not allow you to separate the proclamation from the demonstration. Both are essential characteristics of the gospel, and therefore must be incorporated in the presuppositional reading of the text.

This is the Bible preaching that prepared the church to respond in a greater way to the call of God, but what exactly that would entail none of us actually knew. In Chapter 3, Dr. Canty and I have selected several passages that we were able to view with a new lens that illuminated the text and served as contextual bridges to reach our community.

In addition to biblical preaching and teaching, I had purposely kept our vision statement in front of the congregation which reads: *Our vision is to be the arms of God reaching out to people who do not know Christ personally. We also desire to welcome the children of God, who may have lost their way or who have no church home, to a warm loving setting for which they can come back to God.* I got it out of the passage in Hosea 14:1 MSG which reads: *"O Israel, come back! Return to your God! You're down but you're not out. Prepare*

---

[2] Franke, J. R. (2005). *The character of theology: An introduction to its nature, task, and purpose.* Grand Rapids, MI: Baker Academic.68

your confession and come back to God." This passage in Hosea 14 deals with the people of God recognizing their sin and turning back to Him.

Our church logo pictures hands reaching out to a globe with our tagline, "Come Back to God," which we kept before the congregation to remind them what our mission as a church consisted of. We were not in existence for our own comfort, but to be the tangible expression of God's love to the world.

The Preparation

Prior to 2008, Great Commission Church shared buildings with several existing churches. Because of the small number of members of these host churches they counted on GCC's income to keep them afloat. However, these situations limited our ability to connect with the communities because we had no true roots there and our future and final location was not determined. Due to sharing a building, we had to meet at traditionally off times, as late as 4:00 in the afternoon, which was also a hindrance to our outreach efforts. Therefore, we were in need of a home of our own. The vision of the church and the passion of our membership was all moving toward Philadelphia, so we decided to pray and vote about the idea of possibly moving our church into the city. The vote was unanimous; they voted to move from the suburbs into the city of Philadelphia. But Philadelphia is the 5th largest City in the United States so how do we decide where to go? Obviously, we couldn't just use the *Coming To America* method and just spin the globe and blindly pick.

Why West Oak Lane?

West Oak Lane Philadelphia was identified as the furthest distance to which the church could relocate while retaining the majority of our congregation. How did we come to this conclusion you might ask? We took a close look at our congregation and discovered there was roughly a 65/35 percentage split between suburban and Philadelphian members. However, out of the 65% suburban members almost 50% of them were originally from Philadelphia. But we also knew they all moved or attended church in the suburbs for a reason. They did not want to be bothered with gunshots and the destructive behavior that they identified as city living. West Oak Lane was just across the city line, and not so far into the city where they could not return to the suburbs in 10 minutes, but far enough into the city to witness teddy bears lined up on the corner to memorialize where someone had just been murdered.

The following study and demographic research may not mean much to you unless you plan to serve in the West Oak Lane Community of Philadelphia, however, I included it here so you could know what kind of data you need to examine as you look to build bridges to reach and serve your community.

We did a demographic search of the community to seek true compatibility. This data consisted of, but was not limited to:

1. Employment and unemployment rates
2. Average household income
3. Education status, along with truancy and dropout rates
4. Age profile of the generational percentages of the residents
5. Race, ethnicity and cultural identification
6. Family and household make-up; divorce rates
7. Recreation with social and community engagement identified
8. Faith receptivity and identification with organized religion
9. Crime, both violent and non-violent types

Sixty-five percent of this community was under 46 years of age, mirroring 75 percent within Great Commission's congregation. Therefore, a relational approach to ministry was possible. This statistic was important because the life issues that the majority of this community faced, were also being faced by the members of GCC. Obtaining a mortgage, parenting teenagers, sending children to college, relational conflicts, and single parenting were challenging the members of Great Commission; however, our members possessed resources to help us navigate through some of these issues. The desire was to help our West Oak Lane neighbors navigate successfully through these issues as well.

The median household income in 2006 was below $45,000, and that figure has dropped considerably due to the economic recession. It currently lists as just slightly above $35,000. Great Commission Church is a middle-class congregation, which would seek to financially support the businesses in the community as well as equip and empower the unemployed of the community to become self-sustained. We understood that limited income was normally synonymous with limited opportunities; however, GCC desired to bring services of value to this community to help impact their lives, with no cost to residents.

The educational level of this community was considered very low—26 percent of its adult residents had not graduated high school and only nine percent of the total number of adults in the area had graduated from college. Great Commission has a high level of college degrees within its congregation. The opportunity to impact the educational level of this community mirrored GCC's passion.

The family structures within the homes in West Oak Lane are very non-traditional. Only 35 percent of the families have both fathers and mothers in the home. Fifty-five percent of the families have just mothers and nine percent are made up of just fathers. Great Commission is a family-oriented church, but has a large number of committed men, which has been its blessed trademark. A positive impact by GCC on children who do not have fathers in the home could affect the overall living conditions and future of this community.

A physical hands-on survey of the community was also done. GCC began prayer walks throughout the West Oak Lane community with their eyes wide open, seeking to discover what God would reveal as His will for the church. GCC started interviewing people on the streets, asking them what some of the greatest needs of the community were and if these needs were being met. The members attended community town meetings to hear the complaints and concerns of the West Oak Lane community. The neighborhood newspaper was read to get a feel for residential life and happenings. The pastors began attending block captain meetings to learn about current issues affecting the church's immediate community. GCC members supported and befriended local business owners and sought their input on how they thought the church could have an impact on the community.

We surveyed the residents and discovered their love for the community and their desire to see it restored to its glory days as a well-respected and safe neighborhood. The majority of the complaints and worries of this community were fixated on the hopelessness of the young people and how their state of rebellion was manifested in drug use, drug sales, truancy, armed robberies, violence, teenage pregnancies, and sexually transmitted infections, to name a few.

The most disappointing find was the community's inability to see God working through any of the churches in their neighborhood to help heal some of the conditions the residents were experiencing. This does not mean the churches in the community were not doing anything. It merely reflected the responses we received through our boots on the ground survey. Therefore, in January 2008, Great Commission Church relocated to the West Oak Lane community of Philadelphia.

The Progression

Coming into the city required a willingness to move physically and spiritually. This was a middle-class suburban congregation moving into what was considered a working-class urban community. The physical challenges were not about traveling but about giving up the comforts of a parking lot and perceived safety to now being very cautious of one's surroundings when coming to and from the church. The area was blue-collar and Great Commission's normal dress code consisted of dresses and suits, or at least sport coats. But the Philadelphia community reflected a much more relaxed attire, which demanded change if we were going to relationally connect.

We encountered many challenges upon our arrival into the city. I will share a few of the incidents not to scare you or deter you, but to show you that even when you are doing exactly what God has led you to do, facing opposition is still a strong possibility, but do not let it fool you into second guessing your call.

We moved into the building in January 2008 and a few weeks in, due to some complications with the gas company, we found ourselves with no heat on Sunday morning prior to our worship service. It was freezing cold and even if our members kept their coats on, focusing on the worship would prove to be very challenging. We sent some guys to the Home Depot to grab as many electric heaters as they could and we strategically placed these heaters throughout the sanctuary and prepared for service. But we were also having our first baptism service and we realized the water was off as well. The men had to rush back out and go to Lowes and grab a ton of the five-gallon waters used for fountains and used them to fill up the baptistery. The panic and emotional trauma of not having heat and water put us through it that morning but we persevered through it. God was praised.

The first outreach effort we had since coming into the city backfired on us. We decided to host a Super Bowl fellowship and invited the men from the community to come and enjoy the game on this huge screen television we just purchased. We ordered pizzas and wings and made this a free gathering for one and all. To our surprise and pleasure some men from the community showed up and joined us for the game. However, we discovered when we came to the church the following Wednesday, someone enjoyed watching that big screen so much they decided to break into the church and take it home to watch it some more. The honeymoon and naiveté of us being in the hood was gone and we knew that although we had great big hearts, we must learn to be as wise as serpents and as innocent as doves.

One of the more serious incidents that we encountered was when I was leaving the church one Wednesday evening and a couple of neighborhood drug dealers were sitting directly across the street from the church. I would see these same guys on most evenings as I left the church. On this one particular night, as I stood there with the other men making sure our female members got to their cars safely, I noticed one of the men staring at me. Instead of ignoring his menacing glare I decided to return a threatening stare of my own. This locking of eyes is a hood thing and the winner is the one who refuses to turn away. As it turned out, I won that battle and the drug dealer turned away. I walked to my car with a machismo confidence that communicated *just because I'm the pastor; do not mistake that to mean I am soft or weak in any way.* When I got into my car and drove away, the conviction of the Holy Spirit was overwhelming. It was as if the Lord said, "Really? I put the broken right in front of the door and you decide to become a thug instead of trying to reach them!" Well this conviction from God had me anxious to see these guys again and make up for this embarrassing interaction. I began to pray for them and my interaction with them upon our next encounter.

The following week when I saw these men, I approached their car and requested an opportunity to speak and introduce myself. They nodded to say it was ok, and I began to introduce myself and apologized for not doing so before. I also explained being from North Philly as I am, turning my head when I'm being stared at, does not come as naturally as it should. They were shocked that I would show them enough respect to apologize, and in return they apologized to me. They also said they wanted to thank the church for all it was doing in the community, especially how we took the sons of incarcerated parents to the Phillies game. The encounter with these men scared my wife when she heard about it, but it blessed me tremendously. I never asked these men to stop selling drugs across the street from the church because I figured some more prayer and a few more conversations and, maybe I could get them to come visit the church. However, within two weeks they decided they felt guilty for selling drugs across from the church. They left and have not been back.

Other challenges that surfaced were learning how to welcome and worship with people who were introducing many spiritual challenges that conflicted with the Word of God. We would define a couple as a husband and wife prior to our move in the city, and we had a couples ministry that offered edification and fellowship. However, many of the couples that began to attend the church were simply living together outside of biblical matrimony. We orchestrated a date night and purchased a ton of tickets to take couples from the neighborhood to see the movie *Fireproof,* starring

Kirk Cameron as a firefighter fighting to save his marriage. Following the movie, I did a preaching series discussing the blessings of marriage built on a solid foundation. This led many of these couples to want to join our church, but due to their living together I had to share with them that they would be on church discipline because they were living in sin. However, I added that they were more than welcome to continue coming and even attend the new disciple's classes but we would delay the right hand of fellowship until they were married. I also questioned their hesitation in pursuing marriage and undoubtedly it revolved around the cost of the wedding. This gave me a chance to share I would officiate their ceremony at the church for free which they could do immediately. In addition, I shared they could still have a wedding later when they could afford it and I would do that one as well. I informed them that marriage was for God, but the ceremony was for the people. Honoring God was most important. I can say, by the grace of God, I performed two weddings for several couples who decided to take me up on this offer.

A baby dedication was always a great time at GCC and it did not seem like a controversial subject until it came to unwed parents, unequally yoked parents, and teenage mothers, which is what we had encountered in our new location. We were faced with a dilemma: do we only serve the saved married couples by praying for their babies, challenging them to raise them up in the admonition of the Lord; or do we dedicate all of the children and leave the conviction up to those who participated? Through prayer, we decided to add a third option of having annual prayer for the babies and challenge the entire church to stand and commit to helping these young children become godly individuals. This became our annual tradition.

The greatest progression came in the ministries Great Commission Church needed to offer to the new community we now inhabited. To prepare for this change, we shut down all of the ministries at the church, except for the edification of our members through men's, women's and children's ministries. This opened the door for us to join in on what God was already doing and what He wanted us to do in this new community. Over the past 10 years in this community God has led us to minister to children with incarcerated parents; mentor children at the local elementary through high schools; serve spiritual and physical food to the homeless of the community; start football and basketball teams for the church and neighborhood kids; partner with Young Lives to serve teenage mothers; chair a new work entitled "Community Forgiveness and Restoration" to reduce recidivism by serving returning citizens; annually ministering to our neighbors with Thanksgiving dinner; subsidize the elementary schools' lack of programs for holidays and Black History Month; being first responders to tragedies our neighbors encounter to violence or fires; start ministries to help heal abused women, people struggling with addictions, and "Gone too Soon" a ministry to minister to parents who have lost children to tragedy, as well as those who are grieving traumatic losses.

For those who think they have to go to another country to participate in a mission trip, I'd like to offer an argument that there is much work to do right outside many of our own church doors. We only moved ten minutes from our previous location and our eyes were opened and our hearts were broken for those things that made our Lord look at the city and weep (Luke 19:41). People were lost, broken, and searching for love, healing and prosperity in all the wrong places. Our passion and purpose are to help them to see who can really bring them Shalom!

Table 1 is a sample of the letter our members were given to distribute to their family and friends to help us raise funds to purchase our building in West Oak Lane.

Conclusion

This chapter shows how one church was obedient to the Spirit's leading and followed God into the city of Philadelphia. We were being sensitive to Jeremiah 29:7, "…and seeking the peace and prosperity of the city." (NIV) We understood that Philly was a major hub for the creation of culture, and that its peace and prosperity could lead to the prosperity and peace of others. Although Great Commission Church was primed through the preaching, which we will discuss in greater detail in chapter three, I've had the heartbreaking task of seeing the death of many churches due to their lack of movement outside of their doors. For many of these churches the issue is not moving to a new location but simply moving out into their communities. In chapter two I discuss some of the more common excuses I've encountered, which have led to the majority of churches in North America experiencing stagnation and decline.

Table 1: Sample Letter

August 7, 2007
Mr. and Mrs. John Doe
100 Main Street
Your Town, USA 99999

Dear John and Mary:

I have some very exciting news to share with you! The Lord has given me an opportunity to participate in a missionary trip to the West Oak Lane section of Philadelphia. Yes, you read correctly, West Oak Lane. For centuries we have been sending missionaries all over the world while people in our own communities are dying daily without Christ because many have turned their back on God and His church. With current conditions in the city, I feel called to … (fill in your passion and your giftedness to reach this area)

Along with this wonderful opportunity comes the responsibility of raising both prayer and financial support. I would like for you to take a few moments right now and pray and ask God how you can be a part of my ministry training and experience. As you can imagine, your prayer and financial support are crucial in helping me in this endeavor. I ask that you prayerfully and financially stand with me as I continue to grow spiritually so the Lord may use me more for His purposes. If the Lord leads you to partner with me financially, please know that your money will be used not only for the GCC Vision Fund, but also to help in my spiritual and cultural growth, sharpening me for greater ministry in the future. If you feel led to uphold me in prayer, I will appreciate that also.

A crucial part of my responsibility in loving the city the way Christ does is raising the finances needed to have a physical presence in the community. In order to do this each of us have been asked to raise $2,000, which will go toward purchasing the church building and the adjacent café, which will be used as tools for reaching the community. I ask that you prayerfully and financially stand with me as I continue to grow spiritually so the Lord may use me more for His purposes. If the Lord leads you to help me in this unique opportunity, please send your check (payable to Great Commission Church) and place my name and the phrase "mission support" in the memo section. A receipt will acknowledge your contribution, and it is tax deductible.

Thanks so much for your support and prayers!

Questions

1. The increasing homicide rate was a catalyst for GCC to move into the city. What people group does your heart break for and why?

2. How are you currently seeing your community as a mission field, and what do you believe are the next steps to foster that?

3. What changes does your church need to make to become more missional, and what needs to die in order for a new ministry to be birthed?

4. What church traditions exist in your context that are hindering the engagement of the unchurched and the growth of your congregational body? What can you do to address these?

CHAPTER 2

Resistance To Repentance

In my (Larry) role as a professor and State Director of Healthy Churches, I have had the pleasure of mentoring and consulting with hundreds of pastors. The greatest pain of this privilege is hearing the pastor's discouragement and defeat of not being able to move their congregation from where they are to where they believe God is taking them. This chapter is a mere snapshot of some of the excuses I've heard along with some Scriptures I've used to help equip these pastors to minister to their congregations biblically and missionally.

Let's face it, most Christians understand that someone has to tell someone else about Jesus for that person to accept Him as Lord and Savior, the problem seems to be everyone's waiting on someone else to tell that someone.

Sister Mary (not her real name) for the last thirty years has been seen as one of the most faithful members of the church. She comes to church every Sunday; she's a faithful tither; she sings on the choir; she's an usher and serves as a pastor's aide. She's been a Sunday school teacher, a deaconess, and in her many years of service, she has led women's ministry and hospitality. Brother Craig (not his real name) is also great. He's a deacon, so he opens and closes the church. He leads men's ministry; he's a part of the security ministry, and he's also a very generous tither. In fact, there is not a ministry that calls for a man that Brother Craig probably has not volunteered for. Truthfully everyone loves Sister Mary and Brother Craig so much that they wanted to honor the two of them at the upcoming church anniversary. The church wants to say thank you for all that they do and have done over the many years. So the church decided they would interview them to highlight their many contributions to the Kingdom of God. The first question asked was how many people over their many years of service do they think they have led to know Jesus Christ. The thought was that there would be too many to even count, however, sadly for both of them the answer was none. Astonished by their answers, the question was rephrased to ask. "How many times do you guys think you have personally told an unbeliever about Jesus and then gave them an opportunity to make a decision about their faith?" The answer again was zero. This time however Brother Craig added, we have participated and been apart of a million jobs, but we did not want to take pastor's job, after saying this some laughter erupted from the church. Was that laughter nervous energy due to the discomfort of the those in attendance, or was there a real sense that, yes, telling the lost about Jesus was the pastor's job and how silly to think it was someone else's?

This story is one I created based on the reality that the majority of Christians who spend their lives in church will never actually bear witness of the Gospel to an unbeliever. Somehow being busy with church stuff became the validating factor of one being a faithful Christian. But how can this be the case? Well, this chapter is replete with excuses that have been given in our pews and the pages of Scripture and we must biblically instruct and redirect those following us.

No More Excuses

Excuses are monuments of nothingness; they build bridges that leads to nowhere; those that use these tools of incompetence are seldomly good for anything else.
-Author Unknown

I do not believe there is anything more disappointing and discouraging than to see the bride of Christ, the church, operating outside of the will

19

of Christ. The church, as we discussed in Chapter 1, has a mission and a purpose, and everything we do should flow from that call. Any vision, mission or ministry that conflicts or hinders the mission of God, is simply not of God. Although this may sound simple, I have unfortunately come to discover the exact opposite is happening in many churches.

Preference is defined as *a greater liking for one alternative over another or others.* I have come to discover seven times out of ten, the reason the mission of God is not happening in so many churches today is not because it is not known but because pastors, leaders, and members prefer to do something else. How arrogant and narcissistic it is to think the bride of Christ should be our soul mate on earth to make us happy! I know this may sound harsh, but how harsh is it to kidnap someone else's bride and train her to do what we desire as opposed to doing what He who purchased her with His blood desires? Although the pastor's name may be on the marquee, it's not his church. Although the church might be named "29th Street Baptist," it does not belong to 29th Street.

This chapter is filled with some of the more popular excuses/reasons churches have allowed themselves to be derailed and detained from the mission of God. I want to say I do believe there is a passionate pursuit of purpose happening in many churches, but the problem occurs when we get lost in our preferences. The priority must always be the mission of God, and a consistent evaluation and assessment process must be established to keep our churches accountable.

Excuse: But I've been doing it this way for 75 years

The Lord said leave your country, your people and your father's household and go to the land I will show you. You will be a blessing. So Abram left as the Lord had told him; and Lot went with him. Abram was seventy-five years old

Genesis 12:1, 2d, 4..NIV

Abram had been doing things his way for seventy-five years. He was middle-aged and middle–class and going about his life in his way. But

God decided one day to interrupt Abram's previously scheduled plan with a plan of His own. What we need to see in this narrative is Abram heard from God and changed his way of doing things to do what God called him to do.

Too many churches have been doing the same things for so long they can no longer hear from God. In fact, they seldom even seek God for instruction because repetition only calls for His blessings not His direction. Not many churches will admit that they do not call on God for vision. But when all you do is take last year's calendar and make it next year's calendar and simply change the 75th Annual to the 76th Annual, that is exactly what some of them are saying. This is not to say having annual events are wrong or of the devil, but the mission should drive the calendar not the other way around. This radical movement of Christianity to change the world cannot be placed on the cruise control of our calendars.

So the question to be answered is this: Can a church that has experienced success in the past, that is comfortable with where they are in the present, still hear from God and be willing to change their behaviors to see His will versus their will be done for the future? Abram's faithful obedience is recalled in Hebrews 11:9 and it adds a significant note that really helps us here: "By faith he made his home in the promised land like a stranger in a foreign country; he lived in tents" (NIV). Tent represents a temporary posture, and it carries with it an expectation and a mental preparation to move or change again if the Lord so calls and desires. It's understanding that the church was never meant to be stagnant. She is always going and growing and being refined to continue the work of the Lord. Believe it or not, personal comfort and complacency should never be the goal of the body. If we as older believers are comfortable with everything happening in our churches, then more than likely an unchurched unbeliever would be uncomfortable in that same setting.

Finally, the Lord moved Abram so he could be a blessing. He tells Abram " …all peoples on earth will be blessed through you" Genesis 12:3 NIV. Abram was not being sent just for his own success. The interruption in his life was much bigger than his personal prosperity. All people on earth would be blessed through him or more specifically through his seed, which is Jesus Christ (Galatians 3:16). That's the journey, that's the mission. The church is not in business to bless herself; she's here to bless others. And if we agree, the church exists to bless others. How can we ever justify being so internally focused that we allow her life to be totally consumed with the saved of the church while the unsaved of the community gets less than a tenth of her time? We must be willing to hear from God, move from comfort and interrupt whatever we are doing in our churches to have a greater impact on the Kingdom of God.

Excuse: Who am I to deliver these people?

So now, go. I am sending you to Pharaoh to bring my people the Israelites out of Egypt. But Moses said to God, "Who am I, that I should go to Pharaoh and bring the Israelites out of Egypt?"

Exodus 3:10-11 (NIV)

Moses was living and working in a desert land and the Lord called for him after forty years to go and deliver His people, the Israelites, out of their bondage of slavery. The Lord saw their misery and He heard their cries. God is a promise keeper. He promised to never leave nor forsake us, and it had come time for His people to be delivered. Moses was aware of the Israelites' bondage because he used to live in Egypt. However, due to his own mistakes, his lack of self-esteem, and the overwhelming task God was calling him to, he had to ask, "Who am I that I should go to Pharaoh and bring the Israelites out of Egypt" (Exodus 3:11 NIV).. Ironically, the church may not come out and say it, but the opioid crisis, the homicide rate, the unarmed police shootings, the abortion rate, teenage pregnancy, the recidivism rate, gentrification, the divorce rate, the rise of false religions, the universal acceptance of homosexuality, and the universal rejection of sound biblical teaching have caused the church to be overwhelmed with doubt and fear. In addition, she struggles with insecurity about her God's ability to still deliver His created beings out of their bondage. Many congregations stay in their buildings because they have lost hope that they can do anything about what is happening outside of them. There is a posture of defeat, or even worse, apathy concerning what is happening in so many of our communities.

Gideon cried out to the Lord to say that his clan was the weakest and he was the least in his family. He wanted to let the Lord know that He had called on the wrong guy to stand up and fight (Judges 6:15). But God had to remind Gideon that He would be with him, and with God by his side, he would be the mighty warrior God called him to be.

Small churches often feel like Gideon, we are tucked away over here in our little corner and the mission of God is calling for the mega churches, not us. I believe these are the churches that need to be reminded of how God works. Just ask David about Goliath, or ask Daniel about Babylon, or Joseph about Egypt. We must remember, "Not by might nor by power, but by my Spirit," says the LORD Almighty (Zechariah 4:6 NIV).

On the other hand, some churches think they only have a responsibility to proclaim the Word. So their answer to all that is happening to the people outside the building is to just preach the Word to the people inside the building, albeit in most cases, they're not the same people. There is much judgment and proclamation but very little justice seeking and demonstration. Jesus quotes Isaiah 61 in Luke 4 by saying, "The Spirit of the Lord is on me, because he has anointed me to preach good news to the poor. He has sent me to proclaim freedom for the prisoners and recovery of sight for the blind, to release the oppressed, to proclaim the year of the Lord's favor." He went on to say in verse 21, "Today this scripture is fulfilled in your hearing." In other words, He was acknowledging that these words had been neglected. This jubilee, this justice prophesied, needed to take place and Jesus was here for its commencement. Jesus also says in Matthew 25:35,36, "For I was hungry and you gave me something to eat, I was thirsty and you gave me something to drink, I was a stranger and you invited me in, I needed clothes and you clothed me, I was sick and you looked after me, I was in prison and you came to visit me." And He finishes in verse 40 with, *"I tell you the truth, whatever you did for one of the least of these brothers of mine, you did for me."* Therefore, for any church to believe they have no tangible responsibility beyond preaching to the perils of the people that populate their parish they are totally misguided.

Finally, what we need to observe from Moses is his self-awareness. Moses doubted his oratorical ability, and he asked God to send someone else. God countered with a proposed partnership with Aaron, his brother, and explained to Moses how their teamwork makes the dream work. If we, as the church, could see other local bodies of Christ as partners versus competitors, we could do greater things together than we could ever do alone. The community's depressing statistics, mentioned earlier, would not seem as overwhelming if we stopped focusing internally on our church as a castle and focused externally on the Kingdom of God, of which other churches in the community are a part.

Excuse: That's not really our problem.

Mordecai said to Esther, "Do not think that because you are in the king's house you alone of all the Jews will escape. For if you remain silent at this time, relief and deliverance for the Jews will arise from another place, but you and your father's family will perish. And who knows but that you have come to royal position for such a time as this?" Then Esther sent this reply to Mordecai, "Fast for me. Do not eat or drink for three days, night or day. I and my maids will fast as you do. When this is done, I will go to the king, even though it is against the law. And if I perish, I perish."

Esther 4:12-16 (NIV)

Esther was the First Lady, and living in the castle with the king. The struggles on the streets were real. Genocide and an annihilation of the Jews was ordered, and Mordecai was challenging Esther to do something about it. Esther's responses were very familiar. First she sent clothes to Mordecai who was protesting in sackcloth and ashes and told him to put them on. However, Mordecai's attire represented "Jewish Lives Matter," and he refused to change them. Next, Esther asked what was wrong with Mordecai. It's amazing how she tried to respond to a problem first without even knowing what the problem was. This is something I see the church do often. We respond to what we see, which is often a manifestation of the problem, versus asking the greater question, "What is the problem?" The problem is not the addictions, teenage pregnancies, violence, abortions, hate crimes, etc. These are the *results* of the problem of sin and brokenness. No superficial charity is going to heal this brokenness. Because Esther was removed from the struggle on the street, the idea to send help versus be a help was the natural response.

Unfortunately, many of our churches also operate far away from the struggles of those we are called to serve. We would prefer to *give* a resource than to *be* a resource. "The Word became flesh and blood" and moved into the neighborhood (John 1:14 MSG). [3] If Jesus just gave that message in Luke 4 in the synagogue and left it at that, we could all follow suit. But He hit the streets; He healed; He delivered; He cast out demons; He fed the people physically and spiritually, and we are called to do the same.

Esther went a third step and decided she was going to petition the king on behalf of this situation, knowing it was not popular, knowing it could have cost her, her privileged position and even her life but she still went. It was the king of majority culture who placed them in this dire situation, and it would take the king of the majority culture to reverse the systemic injustice inflicted on the minority culture. There is a call on the church to petition the King. Now we know Esther called for fasting, and we know fasting without prayer is a diet, so we can assume she petitioned the King of Kings, and we definitely need to do that. However, contextually the king I'm speaking of is over the secular government that systematically passed a law that would annihilate a people group.

The church, like Esther, cannot allow her party affiliation to interfere with her godly affirmation. If there are none righteous, then there are no perfect democrats nor perfect republicans. As my good friend Pastor K. Marshall Williams always says: It's not about the donkey or the elephant, but the Lamb that takes away the sin of the world. The church, for far too long, has been a pawn in the political chess game. If we as Christians could recognize the blood that connects us, is of greater value than the

[3] Peterson, E. H., & Peterson, E. H. (2007). *Message bible.* Stl.

socioeconomic racial issues that divides us, we could have some unification in our voice for justification. Micah 6:8 says,"…And what does the LORD require of you? To act justly, to love mercy and to walk humbly with your God." (NIV) What community won't respond to your love and concern and active participation for their relief from the systemic injustices they face? Esther 9 tells us the Jews had a feast and annually celebrated their relief from their enemies and this was all because Esther chose to envision a different outcome than the one being forced upon her people.

Excuse: It's worse out in the world than it's ever been.

He said: "Son of man, I am sending you to the Israelites, to a rebellious nation that has rebelled against me; they and their fathers have been in revolt against me to this very day. The people to whom I am sending you are obstinate and stubborn. Say to them, 'This is what the Sovereign LORD says' And you, son of man, do not be afraid of them or their words.

Ezekiel 2:3,4,6 NIV

Ezekiel's call was not sugar and spice and everything nice. The Lord painted a very clear picture of the people He was calling him to reach. The Lord shared with Ezekiel that the people are stubborn, rebellious, and even in revolt, which literally means they were attacking the Word and the messengers He sent. The idea that everyone is excited and waiting to hear you bring a Word from God, usually is not the case. The church seems to employ a golden age fallacy, which always believes a different time period was better than the one in which they are currently living.

Sin has been here since the Garden, and following this disobedient act, Adam went into hiding, denying and finger pointing immediately. The first family introduced deception and murder, so we need to understand sin has and always will be repulsive and unacceptable to our God. There was never a great period of sinlessness, so we can't make anything great again. This does not mean there has not been some awesome awakenings, remarkable revivals and magnificent movements, but all of these supernatural movements of God came at very dark spiritual times when things just seemed like they could not get any worse. God was summoned by massive amounts of people to enter and engage their world and their lives because nothing else in all the world could change their condition.

The next critical piece of Ezekiel's call was the Lord saying repeatedly to him, "Do not be afraid of them" (Ezekiel 2:6 NIV). This is so important for us as believers to hear and accept. We can't fear the people we're trying to reach. Jesus knew who would betray, falsely accuse, whip, and ultimately crucify Him. However, He still wept over the city. He still had compassion and saw the lost as harassed and helpless, like sheep without a shepherd. He still cried, "Father, forgive them, for they do not know what they are doing" (Luke 23:34 NIV). The whipping, stoning, and martyring of the apostles and the followers of Jesus was always a real possibility from the commencement of Christianity. Brother Paul's words, " ...to live is Christ and to die is gain ..." must be memorized along with, " ...no weapon forged against you will prevail" (Philippians 1:21; Isaiah 54:17 NIV). A theology of success, which does not also include suffering is not biblical theology at all. We must accept we will have trouble, but we can be comforted to know that we will win in the end (John 16:33).

Excuse: To be honest, we really do not like them

Then the word of the LORD came to Jonah a second time: "Go to the great city of Nineveh and proclaim to it the message I give you." Jonah obeyed the word of the LORD and went to Nineveh.

Jonah 3:1-3 NIV

Jonah got the call and ran in the opposite direction. I have heard so many preachers embrace this narrative and relate it to their own run from the call. In fact, I heard it romanticized so much it makes the person who said, "Yes" to the Lord and responded appropriately feel guilty or selfish for doing so. I want to be very clear here. Jonah was being disobedient, period! Jonah 3:3 is the contrast to that earlier disobedience. This time Jonah obeyed the word of the Lord and went to Nineveh. But what I specifically want to highlight in this Jonah narrative is why Jonah ran. Jonah did not run because he was humble, a novice, or not yet ready to handle the call; he ran because he hated the Ninevites.

To be fair there were many reasons Jonah could have given to justify his hatred of the Ninevites. First, it was their ethnicity. They were not Israelites. Second, was their history. They were enemies and were brutal to the Israelites and others. In fact Nahum says about Nineveh, "Woe to the city of blood, full of lies, full of plunder, never without victims!" (Nahum 3:1 NIV) However, none of these issues stopped the Lord from sending Jonah to the Ninevites. In fact, these were the reasons the Lord sent Jonah. Jesus started his ministry telling His hearers to love their enemies and pray for those who persecute you, and finished it saying, "Father, forgive them, for they do not know what they are doing" (Luke 23:34 NIV). His commission was to go and make disciples of all nations (Matthew 28:19). So when we look at how divided the church is along ethnic lines, we have to ask how much of it is due to disobedience.

Now let me be clear; I believe a church should reflect the community where it resides. If the community that a church resides in is 97% African-American, I'm not expecting the church to be a highly multi-ethnic congregation. However, that does not justify all the ministries, foreign and local, being homogenous as well. But what I have found very disappointing, and what I want to highlight here is a church's intentionality in remaining homogenous. The avoidance and the neglect of those we have decided to hate is unacceptable. Let me say this: from Mormons, to Muslims and every cult in between, are mere men that have not heard or accepted the Gospel and are all the same in God's eyes, lost and in need of a Savior. The KKK, Republicans, Black Lives Matter, and Democrats who have not accepted the Gospel are lost. The homosexual and the adulterer who have not accepted the Gospel are lost. The rich and snobby and the poor and indifferent who have not … you get it. Lost! Remember, Jesus came to seek and save the lost. And He says in John 20:21, "As the Father has sent me, I am sending you." (NIV) Therefore, the receiving of the baton to carry on the mission has no bearing on our opinion or agreement with the mission, just our obedience. Ultimately, the Book of Jonah is about holding grudges, hating our neighbors, and running from loving them, forgiving them, and sharing a Word from God with them. But as the community of God, we must strive to grow more to reflect the God of the community.

Excuse: We are just not ready to do all of that yet.

As they were walking along the road, a man said to him, "I will follow you wherever you go." Jesus replied, "Foxes have holes and birds of the air have nests, but the Son of Man has no place to lay his head." He said to another man, "Follow me." But the man replied, "Lord, first let me go and bury my father." Jesus said to him, "Let the dead bury their own dead, but you go and proclaim the kingdom of God." Still another said, "I will follow you, Lord; but first let me go back and say good-bye to my family." Jesus replied, "No one who puts his hand to the plow and looks back is fit for service in the kingdom of God."

Luke 9:57–62 NIV

Jesus knew what it took to live out the mission of God, and he wanted those that followed Him to understand that as well. Jesus needed it to be known His mission was not a prosperity movement; it was a faith movement. He and His disciples were dependent on the generosity of the people wherever they went. He made it clear, following Him was not going to be a road leading to riches. This first potential disciple had to learn there would be rejection and hardship if he was going to follow Jesus, and he needed to know the cost. Unfortunately, churches are so desperate to fill the pews with people that they avoid telling people about the true cost of discipleship. However, if you minimize the cost to your members, then you must minimize your expectations of them. People will count the cost and they may decide it is too high of a price to pay and go somewhere else, but this should not discourage you, as many walked away when Jesus articulated the cost of following Him. If you want true disciples of Christ following you, you must be honest and transparent about the cost and the reward of surrendering their lives to Christ.

The second of the three men in these scenarios asked if he could go and bury his father. Jesus responded, "Let the dead bury the dead," meaning let the spiritually dead bury the physically dead. Although this may have sounded harsh, Jesus needed those that followed Him to understand the urgency of the moment. I have come to discover too many people in our churches spend too much time reflecting on the glory days of old, glorifying when this person was pastor, or when that person led a particular ministry. We tend to glamorize the lives and moments of the past and miss or devalue the lives of those who are still here, and the mission that is taking place. The church cannot afford for her disciples to be consumed with yesteryear and thus neglect working with the living God. Thomas Jefferson said, "I like the dreams of the future better than the history of the past." Paul said, "Forgetting what is behind and straining toward what is ahead" (Philippians 3:13 NIV). The sad reality is unbelievers often see the church as antiquated mainly because she is so disconnected from the present and has no vision for the future because she is stuck putting flowers on the dead.

The final potential disciple in these scenarios wanted to go and say goodbye to his family first. Jesus said, "No one who puts his hand to the plow and looks back is fit for service in the kingdom of God"(Luke 9:62 NIV). Jesus desires to come before anyone in your family (Matthew 10:37), and anything in your life (Matthew 6:33). Peter learned this lesson as he began to sink when he took his eyes off of Jesus (Matthew 14:30). A farmer must make up his mind about the path he is going to plow to prepare the best field, but a distracted farmer could ruin his path and thus not be able to reap the best harvest. Believers today have a very difficult time trying to be in the world but not of it. There is a lust of the eyes which seduces a believer to walk a very distracted life. This formula reduces Christianity down to becoming synonymous with church. And unfortunately, this reflects much of our current culture. Church is tacked on at the end of our very busy week and we call it Christianity. However, if we want to reach the world for Christ, church should start our week and the overflow of our worship would wash the rest of our week with the Word.

Excuse: I've been hurt and I'm not going back.

I appeal to you for my son Onesimus, who became my son while I was in chains. Formerly he was useless to you, but now he has become useful both to you and to me. I am sending him—who is my very heart—back to you. I would have liked to keep him with me so that he could take your place in helping me while I am in chains for the gospel. But I did not want to do anything without your consent, so that any favor you do will be spontaneous and not forced. Perhaps the reason he was separated from you for a little while was that you might have him back for good— no longer as a slave, but better than a slave, as a dear brother. He is very dear to me but even dearer to you, both as a man and as a brother in the Lord.

Philemon 10-16 NIV

Paul's love for a runaway slave and his belief that Christian brotherhood should supersede systematic oppression is wonderfully on display in this letter, and there is a whole lot that can be discussed concerning that in this passage. Specifically, how Paul's understanding of the Gospel is linked to a kind of jubilee for the individual--release from not only spiritual slavery but also physical slavery (Luke 4:18-19). However, the application of this passage I want to look at is Onesimus leaving the house church and his master, who was the pastor, to run for freedom. I think it is pretty clear Onesimus was not a believer when he ran away, and the conditions were as such that he desired to run away. However, Paul it would seem led Onesimus to the Lord and then convinced him to return to Philemon. In addition, Paul appealed to Philemon to receive Onesimus back, no longer as a slave, but as a brother. Onesimus' name means "useful," and Paul uses a play on words to suggest Philemon may have seen Onesimus as "useless." However, he encouraged him to change his perspective on his new brother in Christ because in fact, he found Onesimus to be very useful in his own ministry.

Jesus said, "Blessed are the peacemakers, for they will be called sons of God" (Matthew 5:9 NIV). Church hurt is real, and there are many people outside of the doors, not because they don't believe in Christ, but because they feel they have been mistreated and they have become runaway Christians. Paul recognized how both parties could have fault in his attempt to reconcile Onesimus and Philemon, which is evident in his willingness to pay whatever financial loss the departure of Onesimus may have cost, and the gracious spirit he was encouraging Philemon to possess. The call from our Lord was to make disciples, not just converts. Therefore, we must see runaway Christians as a mission field that need to be prayed for, rescued from their diaspora and reconciled back to the family of God. The unfortunate posture of many faithful church-attending members has been to ignore at best, and gossip at worst about those who have left the body. However, like Hosea being called to go and show his love to his unfaithful wife again and bring her back home, we are called to do the same with the bride of Christ.

Conclusion

Now that we have some of the more common excuses out of the way, in chapter three you will be equipped with some of Dr. Canty's and my favorite passages and some brief exegesis to help move your congregation forward. Remember, moving a church beyond the walls of its building will not happen by might nor by power but by the Spirit of the Lord. Therefore, one has to make sure the preaching and teaching is biblically based and ignited by God's own passion to redeem the lost.

Questions

1. Which excuse does your church identify with the most from this chapter?

2. Why do you think this excuse permeates through your church and what steps are you planning to take to combat this problem?

3. What do you believe are some of the consequences of not rejecting many of the excuses listed within this chapter?

4. What excuse not listed in this chapter have you seen and what passages would you use to minister to those struggling with that excuse?

CHAPTER 3

Pulpit to Pew

Chapter 2 was written to help you deal with some of the popular excuses Christians come up with to avoid placing the mission of God first in their lives. In Chapter 3, We, hope to equip those who have said yes to the mission with a few Bible expositions to help show the relevance of the Bible in ministering in the twenty-first century. The world is changing ever so rapidly, but the church has traditionally been adamantly resistant to change. God is the same yesterday, today, and forever, and His Word is still the most powerful tool we have to minister to His world. However, the approach we use to prophetically and contextually read and apply His Word depends on the audience we are seeking to restore.

Below are a few examples of some of the ills that have recently taken place in the church. The names of the churches have been changed for privacy issues.

At First Baptist of Bedrock, two men joined the church. However, unknown to the church, they were a couple. After six months, they requested the church marry them and communicated they were prepared to sue if the church refused this service that the membership was privileged to.

At Grace International, James, who grew up in the church all his life, demanded people begin calling him Jamila because he believed he was female and he did not want to be identified as male. He believed that God intended for him to be a woman.

At Blackstone, an argument broke out over a seat. One member pulled out a gun and shot the other member, killing him during morning worship service.

At Gabriel AME Church, a young white supremacist murdered nine African Americans at a prayer meeting.

At Saint Mary Cathedral, a man walked down the center aisle, went right up to the presiding bishop who was preaching, and punched him in the face.

The reason I list these tragic stories is because I need you to ask yourself, is you church ready to engage in the trenches of spiritual warfare? Is your church prepared to deal with mental illness, identity confusion, hate, racism, anger, sexual abusers, the sexually abused and the countless other pains and or sins our world is suffering with? As a church, do we ignore these issues, bury them or honestly have no idea how to biblically speak to them? The Bible details our human brokenness from the Garden, and it is replete with fallen characters that were desperately in need of God's restoration. We all would agree, that all of us including you the reader were once a part of the fallen characters in need of a Savior.

My critique of the church could easily mirror a famous line from the main character Doughboy in the movie *Boyz in the Hood*, "Either they don't know, don't show, or just don't care about what's going on in the hood," which reflected how the world neglects those living in poverty. I was wondering how the church could be silent about so much. How do we just continue to sing songs, and do church as usual and tell someone joy comes in the morning, when their child was just murdered and it seems like their night will never end? How do we say time heals all wounds when a father has betrayed a daughter by touching her in a way no child should ever be touched? I'm not saying we should stop praising God because of our tragedies, but I am saying we have to do a better job addressing these tragedies.

This chapter is one of those that could go on forever because of the love we (Kyle and I) have for the Word of God. We individually selected twenty passages and then we came together and chose the ten that was on both of our lists. These are passages we can make more contextually applicable than the traditional ways they may have been previously taught in your context. We do this by applying a missional hermeneutic or interpretation. This section is not meant to be an exhaustive study on any of the selected passages, but rather a more relatable, applicable missional approach that could help you engage the Bible and your community in a deeper way. Our hope is that this study takes you deeper into God's Word as you seek to minister to your context with a greater sense of compassion.

The Missional God and His Scriptures

> When the woman saw that the fruit of the tree was good for food and pleasing to the eye, and also desirable for gaining wisdom, she took some and ate it. She also gave some to her husband, who was with her, and he ate it. Then the eyes of both of them were opened, and they realized they were naked; so they sewed fig leaves together and made coverings for themselves. Then the man and his wife heard the sound of the LORD God as he was walking in the garden in the cool of the day, and they hid from the LORD God among the trees of the garden. But the LORD God called to the man, "Where are you?"
>
> *Genesis 3:6–9* NIV)

The first mission trip recorded in Scripture takes place immediately following the first sin recorded in Scripture. It was God Himself who went looking for Adam, who had instantly become disobedient, lost, guilty, confused, finger-pointing, and most importantly, separated from God. Due to his sin, Adam made a decision to hide from God. Not only was the perfect relationship between man and His Creator fractured, but man's guilt, fear of judgment, and avoidance of accountability caused him to cover up his naked transparency and hide. In hindsight, we know what the damage of this decision by Adam to disobey God meant for the human race, but our omniscient God was fully aware in the moment that this sinful act would cost His Son, Jesus Christ, His life. In spite of that, He still instantly went looking for Adam. What an amazing God we serve. Without hesitation, he went after the one who introduced sin into the entire human race. We can't minimize this significant mission trip made by our God because it gives us our first glimpse of His grace, mercy, and forgiveness. And from this moment in the garden until this very day, God has been on mission to redeem humankind from sin.

When we understand the mission of God, we're more readily able to see how Jesus wrapped Himself in flesh and dwelt among us (John 1:14) and how the Holy Spirit being sent to indwell us (Acts 1:8) are all part of the redemptive plan to reconcile this world to its Creator. We also are able to see how the many characters and circumstances that we have been blessed to learn from in the Bible are not random but were spiritually handpicked for teaching, rebuking, correcting and training in righteousness, so that the man of God may be thoroughly equipped for every good work. (2 Timothy 3:16–17 NIV)

Brothers Killing Brothers (LA)

> *The Lord looked with favor on Abel and his offering, but on Cain and his offering he did not look with favor. So Cain was very angry, and his face was downcast. Then the Lord said to Cain, "Why are you angry? Why is your face downcast? If you do what is right, will you not be accepted? But if you do not do what is right, sin is crouching at your door; it desires to have you, but you must master it." Now Cain said to his brother Abel, "Let's go out to the field." And while they were in the field, Cain attacked his brother Abel and killed him. Then the Lord said to Cain, "Where is your brother Abel?" "I don't know," he replied. "Am I my brother's keeper?" The*

> *Lord said, "What have you done? Listen! Your brother's blood cries out to me from the ground."*

Genesis 4:4–10 NIV

I've seldom heard messages on this passage. Maybe once in a blue moon a pastor preaching a series on Genesis will exegete it, and the focus always seems to major on the offerings of both the brothers and why God found Abel's versus Cain's favorable. However, what I rarely, if ever, hear emphasized is the state of mind Cain was in and how he was obviously disappointed with God's dissatisfaction in him and his offering. The conversation God approached him with emphasized Cain's knowledge of right and wrong, yet his choosing to do wrong affected him. His psyche, being the older brother, was affected by his younger brother, who outshined him in this category.

Finally, we observe how there is no recorded dialogue between Adam and his sons. There is an assumption that there was dialogue prior to the sons' offerings, which is how they were held responsible for their gifts. But what may be more telling, as with Eve's choice to sin, is Adam once again seemed to be nonexistent in the decision-making of his family. Therefore, we discover that although man was created in the image of God, Cain's ability to see himself in this way was gone. He also saw his brother's achievements as somehow an attack on his own. Therefore, as long as someone like Abel was around, Cain could feel less positive about himself. He felt a need to rid his life of this person.

Every day on the news in the city of Philadelphia, we hear about murders that have taken place. Even if it happens outside city limits, there seems to be a strong desire of the networks to find a big murder to be their big story of the day. As sad as that is in and of itself, what is even sadder is the senseless lives that are lost in these unfolding tragedies. But the question is "Why?" I believe this passage can easily show us how the effects of vacant esteem can so damage a person that it can make taking a life seem trivially justified. Dr. Joy Degruy, in her book *Post Traumatic Slave Syndrome,* describes vacant esteem as the state of believing oneself to have little or no worth, exacerbated by similar pronouncements of inferiority from the personal sphere and larger society.[4] In other words, you remove a father's affirmation and you observe others around you with greater success than your own. And on top of that you are critiqued or rightly so even confronted and held accountable, and this fragile person vacant of esteem is now willing to take their own brother's life. In America no person has been more dehumanized than the African-American male. This person has been enslaved, tortured, humiliated, and systematically marginalized by society from the moment he was brought into this country. And the reality is if you tell someone they are worthless, give them worthless education, and worthless opportunities, at some point they begin to really believe they and their fellow man are worthless, and the resulting effect becomes the "Big Story" on the nightly news! However, when you're armed with eyes to see the fragile condition of this man, you don't regard him as a beast, but as an opportunity to minister to him, and become the needed fathers to the fatherless.

Homosexuality vs. The Gift of Celibacy (LA)

Do not deprive each other except by mutual consent and for a time, so that you may devote yourselves to prayer. Then come together again so that Satan will not tempt you because of your lack of self-control. I say this as a concession, not as a command. I wish that all men were as I am. But each man has his own gift from God; one has this gift, another has that.

1 Corinthians 7:5-7 NIV

In this passage, Paul is speaking to married couples where one of the partners has decided to abstain from sexual intercourse. He reminds them that their bodies do not belong to them alone, but also to their spouse. He gives guidelines that if they believe they need to abstain, then make sure they are both on board; they do it for a designated amount of time, and they commit to prayer during this period. Finally, and most importantly, he tells them to come back together so that Satan would not tempt them

---

[4] Leary, J. D. (2017). *Post traumatic slave syndrome: Americas legacy of enduring injury and healing.* Portland, OR: Joy DeGruy Publications. doi:108

because of their lack of self-control. Paul then drops a bomb about celibacy as a gift, which he has. This is no "as a matter of a fact" add-on comment. This gift is what gives him the ability to dedicate his life to the Lord. Not having a natural desire for the opposite sex and a family, Paul refers to it as a gift. And he also communicates that those without this gift who attempt to exercise this abstinence will become a target for Satan.

The Catholic Church has had some very deviant sexual abuse scandals surface that have victimized an estimated 1 million small boys. This abuse is real and the damage unrepairable, but I question if punishing and locking up the culprits is enough? It is obvious that these men do not have the gift of celibacy. It is obvious they failed to exercise self-control. It is obvious they allowed Satan to tempt them. So, when will the Catholic Church stop making this man-made requirement of celibacy a requirement for the priesthood? And in a more general sense, can the gift of celibacy have any relationship to the rise of homosexuality in society in general? Not being attracted to the opposite sex is not a sin; it could actually be a gift. Yet in the perverted satanic world we live in you are ostracized, teased, and forced to think you are different versus gifted. How does this end up playing out? Many times due to the affection and compassion coming from others who have experienced those same feelings of not belonging a common bond of trust and compassion has resulted which has given birth to many homosexual relationships. In this brief practical exegesis I cannot possibly deal with the role of abuse, or absent adults, the X versus Y chromosome debate on being born this way, or the simple preference of people. I'm speaking from a biblical stance about the absence of knowing God and His Word and how that will undoubtedly leave you to your own lustful desire of exchanging natural sexual relations for unnatural ones (Romans 1:21-27). However, I wonder what would happen if we, as a church, recognized this lack of interest in the opposite sex, or even the attraction to the same sex by our members, and instead of ostracizing, finger pointing, or labeling them, we embraced and showered them with the love and knowledge of God. Is it possible that the gift of celibacy could be introduced, nurtured, and a strong soldier and voice for God evolves? Is it possible that even the person who adamantly demands they were born that way recognize that they were born in sin and that God has graced them with an opportunity to be born again? Can we leave the judging to God and demonstrate the loving He called us to do, in order to help with the healing and restoration of these people who too were created in the image of God?

Returning Citizens (LA)

One day, after Moses had grown up, he went out to where his own people were and watched them at their hard labor. He saw an Egyptian beating a Hebrew, one of his own people. Glancing this way and that and seeing no one, he killed the Egyptian and hid him in the sand. Now Moses was tending the flock of Jethro his father-in-law, the priest of Midian, and he led the flock to the far side of the desert and came to Horeb, the mountain of God. There the angel of the Lord appeared to him in flames of fire from within a bush. Moses saw that though the bush was on fire it did not burn up. So Moses thought, "I will go over and see this strange sight—why the bush does not burn up." When the Lord saw that he had gone over to look, God called to him from within the bush, "Moses! Moses!" And Moses said, "Here I am."

Exodus 2:11,12 3:1-4 NIV

These two passages span a forty-year period from Moses murdering a man to his subsequent call by God. During the forty years of exile, Moses was a refugee in a foreign land. He fled from Pharaoh and the death penalty he would have received for his crime. Yet the Lord still chose to use Him. And this forgiveness and restoration of an individual called and used mightily by God is not an anomaly—David, the adulterer and premeditated murderer, Saul the terrorist and murderer, Rahab the prostitute and the list goes on and on. The point is, we can't spiritualize away the freedom of the prisoners Jesus spoke about in Luke 4:18-19.

There is true forgiveness at the cross. Prisoners are not meant to be locked up and the key thrown away. They are to be restrained, reprimanded, and restored so they can return to being citizens again. Any system that profits from storing and enslaving human beings needs to be carefully and consistently examined and held accountable for its service. This does not mean people should not be punished or held accountable for the crimes they commit. However, the church has to recognize God's amazing use of these returning citizens and value the potential these individuals can bring to the Kingdom of God.

I have to pause here and say I am forever in debt to Chaplain Rafael Torres, Dr. Thomas Robinson, Pastor Darryl Dade and Sister Florence Penny McDonald for challenging me to open my eyes to a people that have been forgotten by many in society. I serve as the Chairman of Community Forgiveness and Restoration, which is an assembly of clergy, community leaders and rehabilitated and transformed incarcerated citizens, working together to educate and effectuate faith-base solutions to crime prevention, public safety, criminal justice and prison reform.

Prison reform and programs that attempt to push back recidivism should be important to the church. What is so critical and often missed in the above passage is the amount of people that were left hurting in Moses' absence. I praise God the Lord did not ignore their cry and He sent Moses back to them. Coincidentally, there are many broken families that are never able to recover and pick up the pieces after a mother or father is incarcerated and taken from the home. The community is also impacted perpetually by a system that sees more value in them behind bars than in society. The church needs to be attentive to the cries of these families as well as seek to become fathers to the fatherless, mothers to the motherless, and a source of support to the modern-day widow whose spouse has become figuratively dead to them by their absence.

An Infirmity Hand-Picked by God For You (LA)

To keep me from becoming conceited because of these surpassingly great revelations, there was given me a thorn in my flesh, a messenger of Satan, to torment me. Three times I pleaded with the Lord to take it away from me. But he said to me, "My grace is sufficient for you, for my power is made perfect in weakness." Therefore I will boast all the more gladly about my weaknesses, so that Christ's power may rest on me. That is why, for Christ's sake, I delight in weaknesses, in insults, in hardships, in persecutions, in difficulties. For when I am weak, then I am strong."

2 Corinthians 12:7-10 NIV

This passage has come to comfort me on many days because I see my brother Paul, who is a biblical scholar, an author, a church planter, a faithful missionary, and a hero in the faith being told, "No" repeatedly by God. Paul petitioned God to remove this thorn that he describes as tormenting. Tormenting is defined as a continuing painful mental or physical affliction, an ongoing and never-ending issue. But the Lord denied Paul's request. Why can I find comfort in this verse? Because we need a theology that includes suffering. Not a heresy that says I don't have enough faith to be healed. So many preachers and scholars alike spend time trying to discover what Paul's thorn was—everything from sexually deviant thoughts to epileptic fits and partial blindness. However, if the actual thorn was the focus, God would have revealed it to us. The greater point is the purpose the thorn serves.

After four years of testing, it was finally confirmed that I had cancer. I was praying for four years that it was not cancer. I wondered how God, allowing me to have cancer, could ever be a good thing. I wanted to remind God that I'm the pastor of that church that moved from the suburbs to Philly and consistently challenged them to build up His Kingdom, I'm also serving your Kingdom by helping to oversee these other churches throughout Pennsylvania and South Jersey to be healthier and more evangelistic. Remember Lord, I was the first African-American professor over there at Biblical Seminary, and remember I directed the urban and doctoral programs and spearheaded that move into the city? Remember, I agreed to be the chairman of that Community Forgiveness and Restoration Program fighting back recidivism. And I went on and on about the other areas He has called me to serve, including the most important of all my role as a husband and father. I continually asked the Lord how and why He could allow this to happen to me? And it was this passage that smacked the conceit out of me and ministered to me in a profound way.

Paul's faithfulness and humility to trust God more than himself, his abilities, or his education was so important. Any chronic pain, cancer, diabetes, heart disease, respiratory, or disability one might have can easily become a source of depression and discouragement. However, when we are reminded that God has purpose in everything, it will move our focus from the thorn in our flesh to the thorn in His crown, which was meant to humble Him and mock His Kingship. But we know how that thorn, which seemed to be so devastating merely became a tool in the greatest resurrection story ever told.

Author Tom Elliff in his book *The Unwanted Gift: Hearing God In The Midst of Your Struggles,* describes Paul's thorn as a blessing in its most clever disguise. He goes on to say: "It was through his deep hurt–and the manner in which he contended with this unwanted gift–Paul was transformed from "spiritual superhero" into a humble authentic fellow pilgrim." In short it was his pain and weakness that ultimately enabled Paul to experience his life's greatest measure of God's grace and power.[5]

I've grown to say cancer is either a life or a death sentence; either it takes you to the Lord permanently or it will take you to Him daily. Either way, as with Paul, there is a growing dependency and acknowledgement of the perfect strength and peace of God which we need and must remind others of, after we have accepted His denial of our request to remove the thorn.

Pro-Birth vs. Pro-Life (LA)

Do not be afraid, Mary, you have found favor with God. You will be with child and give birth to a son, and you are to give him the name Jesus. He will be great and will be called the Son of the Most High. The Lord God will give him the throne of his father David, and he will reign over the house of Jacob forever; his kingdom will never end." "I am the Lord's servant," Mary answered. "May it be to me as you have said."

Luke 1:30-33, 38 NIV

---

[5] Elliff, T. (N.D.). *Unwanted Gift; Hearing God In The Midst Of Your Struggles.*: CLC Publications. 40

This is a very familiar passage and normally preached annually during the Advent season. Mary, who was a virgin, pledged to be married to Joseph, became pregnant by the Holy Spirit as announced by an angel. This should not only sound outrageous to those who have heard the story over the last 2,000 years, but please know it sounded even crazier to Mary who was hearing it for the very first time. Yes, it was a miracle, and yes, Mary had to have faith in this messenger of God. On top of that she had to risk losing Joseph, being publicly shamed, and possibly being stoned to death for what would appear to be fornication and adultery. In spite of all this, Mary accepted this call on her life and the life of her child and uttered the words, "may it be as you have said." But how was she so brave and faithful to make such a courageous commitment? I would say the pronouncement of the success of her baby helped her make such a decision. If the angel would have said she was just going to have a baby, even miraculously through the Holy Spirit, but uttered nothing about who the baby would be and the life He would live, would Mary have still risked everything to have that child? I know for many this line of thinking is very uncomfortable, and for some even sacrilegious or blasphemous, but bear with me for a moment.

Every day young ladies are found to be pregnant, not miraculously of course, but nonetheless with a child and with a decision to make. The political world has divided our country based on the decision to keep the child, which is pro-birth, or to abort the child, which is pro-choice. However, the problem with both positions is they neglect the future pronouncement of the child, which is pro-life. The number one common denominator in the highest rate of abortions is not age, but economics. The struggle many young women face is what kind of life will they be able to provide for their unborn children. In order to receive the public assistance needed to help support the child, these women must be unmarried with no father present, which automatically brings division to the family. In addition, the uncertainty regarding the sustainability and the future opportunities this child will have are so grim, the decision to abort becomes a real option. But let's be clear; I am definitely not in favor of abortion. However, what I would like the church to recognize is if we did not ostracize and publicly shame young pregnant ladies, they would not run from the church. If we fought for affordable and accessible child care, health care, counseling, and compassion we could give these ladies plans for a hope and a future. We have to do more than put up picket signs saying no to abortion and voting for officials who say they are pro-birth, but their politics are not pro-life. Once conception takes place, it is a baby, and therefore they should have the right to live. Pro-choice should be the parent's right to give the child up to someone else to parent, not take a life. Every child is a miracle and a creation of God, whether supernaturally like Mary's, or naturally like every other young mother.

A Love for the Disabled (KC)

The king asked, "Is there no one still left of the house of Saul to whom I can show God's kindness?" Ziba answered the king, "There is still a son of Jonathan; he is crippled in both feet." "Don't be afraid," David said to him, "for I will surely show you kindness for the sake of your father Jonathan. I will restore to you all the land that belonged to your grandfather Saul, and you will always eat at my table." Mephibosheth bowed down and said, "What is your servant, that you should notice a dead dog like me?"

2 Samuel 9:3, 7-8 NIV

It is remarkable to observe David's loyalty to his friend Jonathan as well as his respect for King Saul. Both men are no longer with David, and there is no real obligation on David's behalf to remember the line of Saul or Jonathan. God selected David to be king, and both heaven and earth were in agreement. The reality of David's opportunity to rest and simply rule was without question—all of his enemies were crushed. But here is a man of integrity and loyalty inquiring whether there was anyone that he could show mercy to. Ziba, David's servant, brings to David's attention Jonathan's son Mephibosheth. He was described as being, "lame in both feet." He was handicapped, in modern terminology, and dependent on someone else's sympathy and dedication. David does something remarkable—he shows mercy to Mephibosheth when there was no real benefit to him. He extends an act of kindness by giving this man dignity and access to the king. No doubt he would be cared for at David's table, and this would not be a burden.

When we consider those who are important in our society, our culture tells us that those who have wealth, prestige, education, and access to power are deemed important. Those who exist on the margins, especially the disabled, can be quickly forgotten or dismissed as burdensome. We contradict the Scriptures when we assign the prized seating to those with means in our world. The lame, or handicapped, or let's utilize a term that is more appropriate in our day, "differently—abled" are often forgotten. When budget time comes for municipalities to make alterations to buildings to accommodate those who are differently-abled, it is often looked on as an unnecessary expense because our empathy has become non-existent. The reality is that these are individuals made in the image of God, and although the impact of the fall is more acute and observable, they deserve a seat at the table so that they can be heard. Personally, my daughter is one of those individuals who needs another to advocate for her so that she is cared for. My affirmation of her as she navigates a world colored by Autism Spectrum Disorder is critical. My ability to remember her as we go to family events or attend church functions, go on vacation, or whatever it might be is incredibly important. I bristle at people's callousness in regard to what it means to show mercy. It is as if mercy and advocacy for the least of these is another politically correct battle lost. Jesus identifies with the least of these and in fact, puts Himself as the ultimate recipient of service as we go out and serve those who need others (Matthew 25:31-46).

As a church, we have had to think through serving the blind, the sick, and the differently-abled among us. We've come to recognize that words like "retarded" are harmful to the esteem of individuals with learning disabilities and other limitations. There is a learning curve, and change doesn't happen overnight. But we must take notes from our Savior who did not have a problem associating with those who were visually and physically infirmed. We also should not forget those who struggle with emotional disabilities. In the hood we are quick to label folks crazy and reference archaic mythology with regard to how they arrived at their condition. God has called us to serve, advocate for and assign dignity where it is missing in the same way that David did for Mephibosheth.

False Imprisonment (KC)

When his master heard the story his wife told him, saying, "This is how your slave treated me," he burned with anger. Joseph's master took him and put him in prison, the place where the king's prisoners were confined. But while Joseph was there in the prison, the Lord was with him; he showed him kindness and granted him favor in the eyes of the prison warden.

Genesis 39:19-21 NIV

Jacob and Rachel's son found himself on the wrong side of the law. He is in Egypt, serving a man of stature. Even though he has an impeccable reputation, no one can defend him, and he lacks the power to defend himself. At this point in his life, he knew he had some gifts and a bright future because of the visions that he had regarding his future, but also because of his ability to understand and interpret the dreams of others. It seemed that what once was a blessing has now become a curse. His integrity also seemed to be an anvil weighing him down when he was cornered by Potiphar's wife. Joseph is put in jail without a trial, and without an opportunity to defend himself. Where is the justice? It is God's to give and He often uses circumstances and individuals to exact His justice in the earth.

Joseph is not alone in the biblical record; in fact, he is in good company. Jeremiah, John the Baptist, Paul, Peter, Silas, and let's not forget Jesus were all jailed, either without a trial or within a corrupt judicial system. Imagine the anxiety of being innocent, yet accused and judged for something that you did not do. Joseph experienced being judged by his brothers who sentenced him to slavery. Ultimately, God turned Joseph's situation around and raised him to a place of authority.

Within many African-American communities, the prospect of being charged with a crime that you did not commit is all too real. Many black men and women live in fear of walking out the door and possibly never returning. The possibility of being arrested, shot, or killed because of another person's implicit biases is something that we cannot quickly dismiss. As a church, our understanding of God's justice and a sense of communal fairness provides an opportunity where we can advocate for those who are persecuted unjustly. We fully understand that someone can be charged for crimes committed as well as crimes that they have not committed—there are no rose—colored glasses. We also understand that human systems are broken systems because of the Fall, and everything needs to be redeemed, and we understand our calling to be ambassadors of reconciliation.

We preach, teach, and serve through a lens that acknowledges the sinfulness of all mankind. This includes the authorities in power; mayors, council persons, district attorneys, police officers, etc. There is prophetic authority given to the people of God to address matters of justice through an understanding of what it looks like to both love God and love others. One of the best ways that we can support individuals who have been caught up in the system is to provide a loving environment where they are not unjustly judged yet again. The church offers the gift and example of forgiveness through a full-bodied gospel. This may be the very thing that individuals who have been unjustly treated can receive within the redemptive environment of New Testament community.

A Call For Justice (KC)

I hate, I despise your religious feasts; I cannot stand your assemblies. Even though you bring me burnt offerings and grain offerings, I will not accept them. Though you bring choice fellowship offerings, I will have no regard for them. Away with the noise of your songs! I will not listen to the music of your harps. But let justice roll on like a river, righteousness like a never-failing stream!

Amos 5:21-24 NIV

Amos is a messenger of justice. He is also a shepherd and farmer from Tekoa sent by God to bring to light injustice within Israel. Amos faced opposition from the powerful priest Amaziah and King Jeroboam. He brings attention to the unique sin of injustice within Israel, but he also calls the surrounding Gentile nations to account (Amos 1:3-15). They were committing acts of atrocity within their land, but it was not outside of God's view, and He condemns these acts of oppression. Here is a list of atrocities committed by the leaders of Israel:

- Denying justice within the courts (2:7a)
- Committing acts of violence against the defenseless (2:6)
- Sexual violence and incestuous rape (2:7)
- Extortion and bribery (5:12)
- Manipulating scales to overprice goods in the marketplace (8:5b)
- Slave trading (8:6)
- Distorting justice (6:12b)

Things were so bad in Israel that Amos described the injustice being "bitterness" and "poison" (Amos 5:7, 6:12 NIV). Because of this, there would be future judgment in the form of oppression (Amos 6:14). The nation had been in direct opposition to God's purpose for His community. People could not go to the courts and find justice, and they could not expect the king to decide, neither could they go to the marketplace and expect integrity. The young could not expect protection in the home from parents and the elders. They exemplified the opposite of God's kingdom and therefore the only thing left was the pending "Day of the Lord" (Amos 5:18-27 NIV).

God's ideal for society is that justice would "roll on like a river." The Lord says in response to their empty music and song, "Away with the noise of your songs! I will not listen to the music of your harps" (Amos 5:23 NIV). Their religiousness and fancy form is rejected because they had neglected justice within their midst. The image painted by the Lord in Amos is that of a river being constantly refreshed and ever flowing, permeating the land and filling every part of society. This is like language regarding the rule and reign of God throughout the earth. Justice seeks the correction of these wrongs committed, and it goes without saying that justice should show up in the most obscure places.

Through the lens of justice, we, as a church understand that God is deeply concerned with how we treat each other. In fact, the concept of biblical community stresses the imperative of love. This is replete throughout

Scripture. The community where we exist as a church is broken, and so we are always looking for ways to right the wrong or mend the broken. Outlets like small groups provide a micro view of how justice works. We care for and exercise justice at a table where there is equality and respect. We survey our surroundings, and it doesn't take long to pinpoint the broken schools, and the judicial and political systems at work within a community. In a city like Philadelphia, where there is great disparity, the urgency of justice rings loudly—consider the cash bail system, or the unequal education offered within minority neighborhoods, or the disproportionate "stop and frisk" of black males, not to mention the excessive sentencing of minorities for minor offenses. We are a missionally engaged church, and therefore we take seriously these kinds of issues as they show up at our doorstep if we are watching, listening and asking good questions of our community.

God called a farmer and shepherd from Tekoa to preach truth to power. The church can no longer turn its back on a corrupt marketplace where the marginalized are overcharged for things like healthcare, food, and some of the staples of life. Things like political kickbacks, sex trafficking, sexual harassment as well as sexual abuse of minors and abortion ought to cause the church to weep, pray, and stand up against these practices.

The Block is Calling Us (KC)

In reply Jesus said: "A man was going down from Jerusalem to Jericho, when he fell into the hands of robbers. They stripped him of his clothes, beat him and went away, leaving him half dead."

Luke 10:30 NIV

Jesus told a parable to help an expert in the law with his arrogance. The parable centered around the idea of a neighbor being more about actions than association. Jesus wanted to destroy this idea that a neighbor was simply someone who looked like you, and so He inserted a dangerous roadway or block, and an even more dangerous people group. He used two individuals who occupied a high place within Jewish society, the Priest and the Levite. These were the cream of the crop, the best that they had, but they were ineffective at providing a healing touch to the man on the road who had been beaten and left for dead. The Samaritan, who Jews called "dogs" and "half breeds," was the one to stop on the road and rescue this man. The Samaritan took care of him and provided restoration. He asked the expert in the law, *"Which of these three do you think was a neighbor to the man who fell into the hands of robbers?"* (Luke 10:36 NIV). Of course the Samaritan—lesson learned, we hope. Let's go a step further and think through this stretch of road that resembles so many others that have been like minefields within communities.

The road from Jerusalem to Jericho was a 15-mile stretch that included blind spots and hiding places. It was notorious, and for that very reason needed to be cleaned up and redeemed. How many places in the hood resemble this Jericho road—places where lives are taken, where contraband is distributed, and where the homeless live in perpetual disgrace. This is a forgotten and neglected place until tragedy hits. When tragedy hits, such as a child being killed or someone overdosing then, only then, does it make the evening news. There are places where strongholds exist that need to be redeemed. Some corners in Philadelphia have been held for years by drug families.

We are struck by this proverbial, yet real Jericho road where children travel to school and fear the possibility of being hit by stray bullets—these places need to be redeemed for God's glory. We are called to not only address incidents of violence and restore the victim, but to consider what God told His exiled people in Jeremiah 29:7, "Also, seek the peace and prosperity of the city to which I have carried you into exile. Pray to the LORD for it, because if it prospers, you too will prosper." (NIV) The core of incarnational ministry within a given context is to be committed to bringing the shalom of God into that place.

The block is where many of the marginalized within society identify as home. These are those little roads that break off by the hundreds in a place like Philadelphia. What is our role as the church in regards to Jericho Road? Yes, we are called to help the harmed passerby, but we are also called to have an incarnational presence mimicking our Savior and seek to restore the livability of that road. As a church, we have found too many streets uninhabitable, yet people live there. And if we are honest, we have proclaimed, "Be warmed and be filled." We must find our place on the block and not simply be the church on the block. Our gestation period has been too long and we have been negligent. We are to love our neighbor as ourselves, but must also love our context as well and make a safe pathway for those who call it home.

#METOO MOVEMENT (KC)

Bathsheba

One evening David got up from his bed and walked around on the roof of the palace. From the roof he saw a woman bathing. The woman was very beautiful, and David sent someone to find out about her. The man said, "Isn't this Bathsheba, the daughter of Eliam and the wife of Uriah the Hittite?" Then David sent messengers to get her. She came to him, and he slept with her. (She had purified herself from her uncleanness.) Then she went back home. The woman conceived and sent word to David, saying, "I am pregnant."

2 Samuel 11:2-5. NIV

Joseph

One day he went into the house to attend to his duties, and none of the household servants was inside. She caught him by his cloak and said, "Come to bed with me!" But he left his cloak in her hand and ran out of the house. Now it happened one day that he went into the house to do his work, and none of the men of the household was there inside. She caught him by his garment, saying, "Lie with me!" And he left his garment in her hand and fled, and went outside

Genesis 39:11-12 NIV

Tamar

But he refused to listen to her, and since he was stronger than she, he raped her.

2 Samuel 13:14 NIV

Too often current trends seem novel, but when we examine the Scriptures we see that Solomon says, " ...there is nothing new under the sun" (Ecclesiastes 1:9 NIV). The Me Too movement kicked off in 2017, however, the need for advocacy has been around for ages. Those in power have used their power to take advantage of those under them. Joseph experienced being harassed for sexual favor by Potiphar's wife, King David used his power to take advantage of Bathsheba, and Amnon raped his sister Tamar. In the midst of these violations were enablers, and individuals who provided cover for the perpetrators to do what they did without impunity. Potiphar enabled his wife, David's court enabled him, and Jonadab and David himself enabled Amnon. These individuals were accused and used for pleasure and justice was denied for a season, but God determines when and how he will enact judgment. God's justice is executed either in this life or in the life to come.

Sexual harassment is dehumanizing for the victim. It communicates something about the lack of value one has for another, and it violates God's expectations that love, humility, and integrity characterize our relationships with one another. Predators prey on the vulnerable, and in contrast the church is specially gifted to take up the cause of the weak. We recognize this in Jesus's ministry as He deals with many of the marginalized. Jesus validates women repeatedly throughout his ministry, such as the woman at the well in John 4:1-26. He also validates the least of these; children in Matthew 19:14 and Luke 10:15, the disabled in Luke 14:12-14, and the Samaritan woman in John 4. This fits with a kingdom ethic that requires equal standing among all under the New Covenant made possible through the blood of Jesus Christ (Galatians 3:28).

As the church, we must spearhead the move to do no harm to those who have been harmed. There are women who have experienced violations of their emotional well-being and are dealing with the traditions developed out of a misogynistic culture. Too often the church has given cover or enabled abusers to operate with a wink and a nod, but this violates the summation of Scripture to love God and love others (Romans 13:9). Not only are we called to not participate in covering sin, but to also have a role in advocating and healing the broken parties (Matthew 18:15-19).

The church is being watched to see how we handle instances where individuals come and seek help. Are we dismissive? Do we have a system in place to report immediately? Are we biased in our dealings? God will hold us accountable for the damage we inflict on those seeking help.

Conclusion

This brief journey through these specific texts of Scripture provides a glimpse into our world through the lens of the ancient world. As we progress we are drilling down into praxis, the very practical world of ministry where the specifics of logistics becomes the focus. We share out of real world experience, not contrived principles developed outside of a given ministry location. Context matters when it comes to ministry and we sought to provide a retelling of joining God's mission. The next two chapters chronicles three years of practical ministry. Whereas this chapter was a dive into the people of God in the word of God, the next two chapters chronicle the people of God in the mission of God.

Questions

1. With a missional lens to see the true practicality of Scripture, what Scriptures came alive to you like never before and why?

2. What passage (s) not highlighted in this chapter has the Holy Spirit illuminated to you that may have a direct impact on your ministry?

3. How might a missional lens impact teaching, preaching, and counseling sessions within your local fellowship?

4. To prepare your mind prior to applying a Bible passage missionally ask yourself: What are my presuppositions based on my identity (e.g., gender, age, education, economic class, political affiliation, etc.) Discover which individuals that I identify with within the passage and why? Is there a cultural or physical boundary crossed within the text?

CHAPTER 4

From The Church To The Community

Training for the Trenches

In previous chapters we shared the story of Great Commission Church, and addressed the many excuses that people hold close, and we have equipped you with some Bible to help serve those you engage with on a daily basis. We want to now dive into the "how." This chapter details the training that you would take your church through to reach the community. We suggest doing this training over a 12-week period prior to releasing participants into the community.

Executing a Missional Strategy: Training

The process of developing a strategy to facilitate change within our community (West Oak Lane) took shape in the form of training members of Great Commission Church. We called this 12-week training, "Training for the Trenches" (T4T). Larry and I facilitated the training, which consisted of a seminar-styled instruction coupled with congregational engagement. There were other elements introduced to help participants develop a more concrete understanding of strategic engagement of the West Oak Lane community. We were keen to use things like video, role play, scenarios and other tools that would help deliver new concepts. We began in the fall of 2015 and focused on the adult members of Great Commission Church. This training culminated in fieldwork followed by a public presentation carried out by teams organized for execution within the community. This chapter presents steps to take in order to move forward as real world participants in the mission of Christ. We are beyond excuses and are focused on execution.[6]

As you read through this chapter please recognize that not everything you read is going to be transferable but we will try to be intentional in making suggestions that may help local congregations. Please understand that we are not proposing a cookie cutter ministry model but instead providing some observations that we have come across in our work of missional engagement.

Spiritual Formation Training

As you begin this portion of the training we believe that a syllabus would be helpful to guide the training process. The syllabus should elevate the level of expectation for anyone attending. Although the course is for laypersons, we believe that it is vitally important to 'raise the bar' and lay out clear expectations. We envision that education will lead outside the classroom and into the context to engage the residents of the community. We suggest conducting a church-wide push for registration and ultimately gathering a list of individuals that are on board for the journey. The development of the syllabus should focus on personal growth coupled with a missional commitment to reach the church's immediate context. The framework for the syllabus should include assignments and tools that guided those enrolled through the need for personal growth. The spiritual formation emphasis allows the trainers to incorporate the following resources into the class dialogue:

1. *Good to Great* by Chip Ingram[7]

---

[6] Canty, D. K. (2017). *Developing and implementing a strategy for gospel-centered social change within the West Oak Lane community.*

[7] Ingram, C. (2007). *Good to great in God's eyes: 10 practices great Christians have in common.* Grand Rapids: Baker Books.

2. Twelve Questions Every Believer Must Ask Themselves:

1. What is my calling or purpose?
2. What are my spiritual gifts, and am I exercising them in my ministry?
3. What are my personal strengths and how can I use them to bring glory to God?
4. Have I identified my growth areas and how do I plan to compensate for them?
5. Am I perpetually pursuing a deeper relationship with the Lord?
6. Am I being discipled?
7. Am I committed to making disciples?
8. Do I see people as Jesus sees them?
9. Is my integrity reflective of the character of Christ?
10. Is my servant-hood reflective of the character of Christ?
11. Am I seeking the Lord for vision and direction?
12. Am I moving people onto God's agenda?

We designed these two lessons to happen within a 50-minute designated time slot. The book *Good to Great* is utilized to highlight the need to rise above mediocrity. There shouldn't be an expectation that those enrolled would read the book, but an instructor could simply present the findings within an engaging format. The slides for Twelve Questions Every Believer Must Ask Themselves takes aim at some of the hurdles that hinder believers from being used by God. The seminar format allows for versatility and the potential for engagement around relevant topics. In addition to the two lessons, there are other tools used to help with individual development. Here are some additional items that should be included within the personal growth assignments:

1. Sounds Like Me
2. Half Day of Prayer
3. Spiritual Gift Test
4. Personal Improvement Project

These tools are focused on self-disclosure as a key part to spiritual development. If an individual is fully aware of their individual gifts and talents and are practicing various disciplines, then the hope is that they will feel fully empowered to fulfill God's calling in their lives. The tools are great if they are used by those committed to the process. There is a real opportunity for individuals to take giant steps forward in their personal walk if serious effort is taken to complete the assigned exercises.

The Sounds Like Me assignment requires participants to select someone from the Bible who best reflects their personality, gifting, and their perception of their calling. The goal was for participants to identify with a biblical character other than Christ to help them in their spiritual journey. In past training exercises, there were some interesting biblical characters selected by groups and overall this has proven to be a fun and encouraging exercise full of self-discovery. In addition to the Sounds Like Me exercise we encourage the Half Day of Prayer. If needed, we have provided a Sample Half Day Prayer Guide (APPENDIX A). The prayer assignment introduces a new spiritual discipline into the life of participants and can be a catalytic event. The prayer exercise is designed to challenge people to pull away from the busyness of life and to spend quality uninterrupted time talking and listening to God through Scripture and prayer. We required a minimum of four hours. You will discover that this may be the first time that many participants have engaged in uninterrupted time to this extent in prayer but our hope is that this is a start of a new life discipline.

Regarding the Spiritual Gift Test[8], it is important to understand that the results of this test does not determine whether we participate in the mission but rather it helps us to understand where we fit within the mission. You may find that many participants have already taken the test. If participants have already taken a spiritual gift assessment in the distant past we suggest that they retake an online test. This will remind and reassure your people of what God has deposited in them and the call to be a steward of His gift.

---

[8] Here is a link to an online spiritual gift test that Great Commission Church has used in the past. https://gifts.churchgrowth.org/spiritual-gifts-survey/

The Personal Improvement Project assignment will require more time and thoughtfulness. Here are the parameters for that particular project. Participants should select a problem in their life to work on improving and be prepared to communicate their findings in an essay to the pastors and/ or leaders in week 12. Here are the steps:

1. Choose an issue to work on after prayerful and careful thought
2. Describe the problem in some detail
3. Study the Bible and record relevant insights
4. Set specific goals that will register change
5. Enlist a few encouragers and prayer supporters
6. Log your progress each week in a journal
7. Summarize and comment about what progress you have made and what you will do differently in the future

Expect fruitful conversations around many of the personal issues that rise to the surface because of this assignment. The instructor can utilize this particular exercise as a kind of cumulative project. Overall, this phase of T4T seems more of a primer for what lay ahead.

The use of these tools and similar tools are really designed to help believers discover how they uniquely fit into the body of Christ. The hope is that those you are leading through this training will experience a real excitement around new possibilities coupled with new spiritual disciplines designed to help them grow up in Christ. My suggestion is to take time to honor participants as they share the results of a spiritual gift test or even testify about their time completing a Half Day of Prayer. I would encourage those leading these trainings to be gracious and sensitive to others' experiences. The Personal Improvement Project tool will provide pastors and leaders with a great opportunity to encourage those sitting on the fence in regards to serving. The simplicity of the Personal Improvement Project is to select an area of life that needs attention and put a plan into action to overcome the obstacle. Accountability is built into this particular project as individuals will need to complete this task within community. There is always room for creativity as you lead out on these projects.

Missional Formation Training

This training is going to be contingent on your personal acceptance of chapters 1 through 3 and your ability to articulate what it means to be missional. The next phase of training focuses on developing outreach skills. In this module, you will seek to establish an external presence within your context. You will be pressed to make clear what it means to be "sent people." You will need to be prepared to answer questions and re-explain concepts that will be new to the hearer. As with any foundational truth supporting a community of people, there is always a need to clarify and further apply how this operates in the real world.

In this seminar setting you will also want to elaborate on what it means to be an incarnational church within your context. Please spend as much time there as necessary. The reaffirmation of the missional foundation will be an important step. It will be sobering to observe the lack of understanding and awareness that often accompanies the reintroduction of foundational truth around what it means to be missional. Please do not grow weary in retelling the biblical missional narrative.

In addition to this book, there are a number of other resources focused on what it means to be the sent people of God. We have listed some in the bibliography and you can find others on the website for this book, "www. askmewhychurch.com". Please do not become overwhelmed at this point as we hope to equip you further in a missional understanding over the next two chapters.

The development of a culture centered around being a sent community will look different depending on context. There are no rigid timed stages for missional transformation. We recommend that you give yourself time as you chip away at the things that congregations hold dear. Discussing what it means to be missionally engaged may sound like a simple task but in reality walking with a group of people through a missional turn may be one of the most difficult ministry assignments that exists.

Ask Me Why I'm Not In Church

Missional Community Teams

In an effort to develop strong missional teams we encourage moving toward gathering individuals into groups. The groups provide an opportunity to establish leadership and a team atmosphere as training goes on. These groups will ultimately provide the platform for real world execution. The first assignment within this module includes taking the Community Intelligence Exercise (CIE).

The CIE gives churches a raw assessment of what they know about their community. The tool was developed to help traditional churches do an initial assessment of themselves to see if they are missionally engaged.

CIE Tool

1. Please describe the last time your fellowship addressed a crisis within this community?

2. Who is the city council representative for this community?

3. Who represents this community on the state level?

4. How would you describe your relationship with your church neighbors?

5. Please name the schools within two miles of your church.

6. Identify the nearest recreation center to your church.

7.   Identify the closest shelter to your church.

8.   What is the greatest felt need within this community?

These questions are designed to create awareness among participants. These questions will capture whether the individual and/or church is aware of the many challenges facing the community. In order to operate an incarnational ministry, there is a need to be acutely aware of key places and people within the community. This exercise, along with others, are designed to establish a runway for community engagement. If community change through gospel words and deeds is the goal, then engagement is going to be critical.

How Does the Community Perceive the Church?

As we moved from the suburbs to the city, we quickly became aware of the reputation of the church in this community. We found ourselves navigating a poor reputation and mistaken identity. As a church, we spent much time and energy trying to correct the damage done by the local church in our new space. This required being intentional about serving without an expectation of anything in return. It also required a renewed empathy to the plight of our new community. We rolled up our sleeves and went to work because we lived in a time when the church's past reputation did not necessarily open up doors—instead many doors were closed.

What I described is the struggle that the church in America deals with whether we realize it or not. **_Christendom_** is a term used to convey a time when the church was the center of society and clergy had a voice and respect simply because they were from the church. These times are gone and the paradigm shift globally shows up in the everyday life of churches like GCC. We are trying to reconnect and overcome deep-seated feelings of disconnection that exists in neighborhoods all over Philadelphia and cities and towns in North America.

The *missio dei* or mission of God is a call to re-engage and re-establish a missional/incarnational presence where God has placed us. This requires establishing a new narrative and a fresh application of the gospel within places long forgotten. A cornerstone of this training process includes these missional foundations.

One of the critical pieces touched on in this particular module is Reggie McNeal's instructions on how a church transitions toward missional praxis.[9] The three changes to church culture that McNeal posits are:

- From internal to external in terms of ministry focus
- From program development to people development
- From church-based to kingdom-based in terms of leadership agenda

The class should be designed to go through a set of modules created to be more engaging and dialogue driven. We suggest some videos that will help to facilitate discussions related to missional praxis within context. The "Very Brady Sequel" YouTube clip presents a metaphor for how traditional and entrenched religious practice can hinder gospel witness within a changing culture. The clip shows the Brady family donning their 70s clothes decades after going out of style. In the clip Mrs. Brady had been kidnapped and the response of the kids was to sing a song to make them feel happy. The paradox is that the singing did nothing to help rescue Mrs. Brady but simply provided a momentary emotional escape. It's worth noting that in this scene a Nun is the only one rocking back and forth along with the Brady kids while others in the scene were disinterested and annoyed. The video highlights how traditional ways can create stagnation.

The next video that we suggest presents one of the more popular videos from Rob Bell's NOOMA series. It is designed to intentionally hit hard on the non-relational *Bull Horn Guy*.[10] This video displays a disengaged preacher

[9] McNeal, R. (2009). Missional renaissance: changing the scorecard for the church. San Francisco, CA: Jossey-Bass.
[10] (2011, April 23). Rob Bell - " Bullhorn Guy " Nooma Response. Retrieved January 16, 2017, from http://www.youtube.com/watch?v=M2WopYbO9rQ

who attempts to engage the culture in the most awkward manner possible. Bell positions himself in a favorable manner against the stuffy, irrelevant communicator. The *Bull Horn Guy* has no chance in this characterization. This video can provide some fresh congregational discussion. While we do not endorse Rob Bell's theology, we believe that the video provides fodder for discussion.

The *Madea Goes to Jail* YouTube clip is intended to be the most challenging video because it will stretch the theology and conscience of many in attendance. This particular clip focuses on the controversy of a minister handing out condoms, clean needles, and food vouchers to sex workers. The act of handing out condoms and needles was intended to create a struggle of conscience, and the discussions that follow are rich. The prevailing question is, how far would one go to reach another person on the margins?

As a compliment to the *Madea Goes to Jail* clip, we suggest the TED Talk presented by Jeffrey Browne entitled, *How We Cut Youth Violence in Boston by 79 Percent.*[11] This particular clip provides an insider's view of life within an at-risk innercity community. In this clip, a Boston-area pastor presents a transparent picture of a church's struggle to quell youth violence. An important point presented by Pastor Browne was that his journey required that he became a student of his community. For Pastor Browne, the context became the learning lab; here he adopts a missional/incarnational approach to reaching his community. Although he does not mention the terms missional or incarnational, his intervention resembles missional work. This clip could be presented as an introduction to the preceding three videos.

We briefly touched on establishing teams earlier but I feel a need to reiterate the need for teams. The team dynamic allows for collective prayer, action and support. The teams are micro-communities that go after the macro-community. We strongly suggest not skipping over this part of

---

[11] Brown, J. (n.d.). How we cut youth violence in Boston by 79 percent. Retrieved January 16, 2017, from http://www.ted.com/talks/jeffrey_brown_how_we_cut_youth_violence_in_boston_by_79_percent

training. We found it to be a key kingdom strategy to be apart of and involved in a team.

The video clips selected and highlighted are contextually relevant. If you utilize video please attempt to go for relevance in the eyes of your audience. It will be important to write out your rationale around using a clip so that it can be succinct in your mind, which will in turn address any confusion in the minds of those you are teaching.

Apologetics

One of the critical elements of this phase of training includes urban apologetics. It is important to be prepared to address issues prominent within your community. In the West Oak Lane community we had to address issues such as the presence of Mormonism, Black Hebrew Israelites, Jehovah's Witnesses, Nation of Islam as well as other rising elements of the Black Consciousness movement that were prevalent. The goal of this portion of the training is to develop a starting point in order to understand and to help build bridges to evangelize for the purpose of redeeming them and not simply attacking them. We invited Dr. Derek Cooper of Missio Seminary (formerly Biblical Seminary) to present on World Religions to the congregation.

We were privileged to be able to bring in an expert in the field. I understand that this may not be possible for all churches. There are tons of resources online as well as in book form that may aid in putting together an overview of world religions. Through conversation with Dr. Cooper we were able to help him contextualize the material he presented. We wanted a presentation that was relevant to where we were located. This part of Training for the Trenches can be invaluable to a church's ability to reach community members of different faiths.

Training for the Trenches Project Teams: Missional Praxis

The next phase of the project moves toward real world application. The training should have a window of about three months and is designed to allow for immediate impact on the field. This translates to 12 weeks in preparation and 12 weeks in the field. The earlier teams are formed the more ready they will be to put into action their training.

The benefits of organizing teams early will hopefully avoid unnecessary conflict and personality parity. If your church already has small groups, this may present a natural composition for teams during training as well as in the field. We would not suggest one way to organize teams; in fact, you may want to do an impartial count off to form teams.

One of the first tasks of the team is to establish leaders along with a scribe; this is someone tasked with recording progress for the overall team during weekly outings. It is inevitable that groups will be composed of individuals at various levels of spiritual development. One of the early assignments for groups is to select a location within the predetermined radius around the church building location. We would suggest designating an entire Sunday class to determining summer locations.

A big benefit of a team dynamic is the leadership development as well as the growth experienced due to being in community working toward a goal. The teams are first tasked with organizing themselves and establishing names. Once the task of naming teams and ensuring that everyone understands the protocol, the next task for leaders is to collect shirt sizes for project T-shirts.

The T-shirts represented a key strategy to reach individuals within the separate locations, which were within one to two miles of the church.

I cannot overstate the benefit of teams and/or small groups working together to advance the kingdom in communities. As you consider your community and congregation you will need to determine what is best but my observation is that small groups can provide a nursery where dynamic ideas come to life. Creating and utilizing small groups may require additional time and energy but they are one of the greatest ways to catalyze your people toward a goal.

The Strategy

We encourage you to plan to place teams into the community to execute the missional call, which includes three strategic moves. The first step in the implementation process is the use of a T-shirt as a conversation starter. The T-shirt is a catalyst designed to initiate street level engagement. The second step, be sure to establish a time of engagement. This is important because of the need to obtain maximum participation of members and those enrolled in the training. Third step, establish locations within your immediate context. This will be a critical step to reach your community with some of the tools and missional principles obtained over months of training.

Strategic Step One: Initiating Conversations: T-shirt.

The objective of the fieldwork is to engage your context. The concept of an individual wearing a T-shirt with a message will be the catalyst for engagement. It would also be a reminder to participants of their missional call outside of the church walls. The tagline of the T-shirt would read, "Ask Me Why I'm Not In Church" with your church's web address. The design is purposefully simple in order to obtain maximum attention.

T4T Project T-shirt: *Ask Me Why I'm Not In Church?*

The members of your team can wear the shirt in the field and they should be prepared to answer key questions. The following are examples of answers to the question on the front of the shirt:

1. We believe that we're supposed to love God and love people, so we are out here right now to just show love and concern for people and we'll be going into the building at 11:00 to show our love to God.
2. Our church believes in loving and serving our community, and so we are out here during the summer just trying to really get to know our community and to pray for or serve whomever God sends our way.

3. We are the church, and sometimes the church buildings can be intimidating if you've never been in them. You might wonder to yourself, "What are those people like?" "Will they judge me when I come in?" All kinds of thoughts and stereotypes are made so often about the church. If we never come out of the building, we can't ever help people see we are just a loving, caring group of people sold out for God and this community.

It will be obvious that although trained in how to respond to inquiries about the T-shirt, there will be a real need to further engage around the topic so that participants feel more comfortable in the field. The training includes material that will assist the teams in gospel sharing.

The *3 Circles: Life Conversation Guide* produced by LifeWay Christian Resources is a helpful guide for inexperienced participants.[12] This particular guide uses a relational starting point where individuals can begin a conversation toward a gospel presentation.

Strategic Step Two: Sunday Fieldwork

The evangelism strategy for many churches within the urban context has not changed over the past twenty to thirty years. There are many churches, para-church organizations, and individual believers who have sectioned off outreach to a weekend event. Traditionally speaking, the event would have a big name at a large venue. Believers would invite unbelievers so that they could hear the Gospel message. In contrast, the T4T project will intentionally place individuals at key locations in the community on every Sunday morning for two to three months. The Sunday time slot allows for greater participation. The attendance numbers will vary during the summer months, but the Sunday time slot works with schedules already attuned to worship attendance. Groups would meet in the field at predetermined locations at the stated time or earlier in order to maximize impact. We would encourage consistency with the time and place as this

---

[12] 3 Circles: Life Conversation Guide | Life on Mission. (n.d.). Retrieved November 30, 2016, from http://lifeonmissionbook.com/conversation-guide

would remove confusion and cut down on fear of the unknown as the project progresses.

In addition to Sunday fieldwork we have found it advantageous to include Wednesday evening as a day designated to pray over these locations. Praying over locations as an act of preparation for engagement is a critical step. This step exemplifies an attitude of trust and dependence, as we understand that the work cannot go on without the Lord's intervention.

Strategic Step Three: Location

The designated number of teams should be tasked with finding a location within the proximity around the community in order to establish a station for the summer months or whatever season is determined for the fieldwork stage. The selection of these locations would be critically important because it would allow team members to gain trust with business owners, civic establishments, and others who frequent these establishments. The process of showing up week after week would provide the bridge, which in itself would be the strategic point of connection. The consistent presence of the teams at their location, along with a visual identifier ("Ask Me Why I'm Not in Church" T-shirt,) creates familiarity, especially with business owners who might otherwise be leery of loitering.

The separate locations should be within the context of the church. This allows each team to connect with a business, whether it was a restaurant, convenience store, laundromat, or coffee shop. The teams should be tasked with connecting with the business owner or manager upon the initial visit to the assigned location.

It is important to remember that the business owner represents a stakeholder, someone with a long-term view on the location. An obvious distinction should be made between business owner and manager. At an establishment like McDonald's a relationship with a manager may not yield long-term dividends, however, establishing a relationship would still be necessary for teams to set up at this location. The benefits of these business connections will be elaborated on in Chapter 5.

As you research locations think in terms of the traffic that would automatically flow to these teams. Consider supermarkets, food stands, bodegas, hair care stores, laundromats, cafes, pharmacies, child care facilities, gas stations, etc. Training for the Trenches teams are assigned to reach out to these establishments and create a relational bridge.

The excitement of moving out into your community is being able to create a strategy for reaching that community. The phenomenon of reaching new places and people groups should drive us to new levels of creativity. The work of contextualizing ministry is good work that models what we observe in the Gospels and the book of Acts. There is nothing wrong with strategy as long as we understand that it may change depending on how the world changes around us. A strategy is simply another tool to fulfill the mission that we have from Christ.

Survey Tools

As you prepare to launch Training for the Trenches consider the following surveys created and utilized exclusively for the execution phase of the project. The primary tools were designed to elicit the interpersonal and team dynamic prior to going out into the field, within the field, and then the subsequent debriefing. The following is a list surveys provided to team leaders and T4T participants:

1. T4T Representative Survey
2. Community Location Survey
3. Group Dynamics Survey
4. Conversation Survey

Training for the Trenches Representative Survey

The Training for the Trenches Representative Survey (Appendix B) focuses on the individuals and their level of preparedness for this project. The questions relate to team member's previous experience engaging in public evangelism. We provide no rubric but feel free to establish a standard for how you will categorize results.

As a leader, you should be prepared for various responses to this particular survey. This tool will help to give a preview of those with you heading into the field. The importance of this questionnaire is that it establishes a baseline to compare and contrast with a post project assessment. This is where growth could be gauged and measured. One of the great takeaways from this survey is that as an instructor, we need to be prepared to equip those heading into the field overcome barriers to public engagement.

The second question on the survey (APPENDIX B) is designed to evaluate the experience level regarding relational evangelism. If you decide to utilize this particular survey it will be helpful to dialogue about it within a training class. The content of the dialogue can become fruitful for future trainings and follow-up.

The question related to personal barriers will provide insightful responses from participants. The last question within the survey is open-ended and designed to explore, prior to the project, the impact one believes the gospel will have as they venture into their context. This question will allow participants the opportunity to share their feelings regarding the effectiveness of the gospel.

These preliminary questions are key for churches looking to disciple individuals through missional transformation. It should be noted that this is not an exact science, but the fruit gained from knowing where a congregation is on the missional continuum, and then look back and observe real growth is invaluable. As pastors and leaders, being able to observe pre-fieldwork and then contrast that with post fieldwork is something to rejoice about.

Community Location Survey

This particular survey was created to determine the reasons why teams would choose a specific location. This survey (APPENDIX C) will provide a description of the location as well as identified opportunities to serve at these locations. The selection of the location is a critical transition because it gives direction to existing plans. As you work with participants give some pre-project criteria so that teams will be able to establish a locale worth committing to for the eight- to twelve-week commitment over the summer months. The radius should be a 1-2-mile circle around the church.

The second question requesting outward/visible signs of brokenness that you see within your location was designed to connect the spiritual to the physical. Another way to communicate this question would be the following: "Is the spiritual brokenness within the world connected to the social decay of a community?" Here are some of the kinds of responses that you could receive from this question:

> *"The outward sign of brokenness are homeless people. One man was sleeping on the church steps."*
>
> *"Our kids are popping pills and it's becoming an epidemic."*
>
> *"We observe mental illness, addiction, lust, homelessness, drugs."*
>
> *"Jesse, was an addict sitting on the church steps."*
>
> *"A prostitute is with her client—trying not to connect with us."*
>
> *"Generations of people glued to their phones neglecting human contact."*
>
> *"Young and old with bright futures are taking their lives."*
>
> *"A young man, 34-years-old, said that he was raising his three children with his mother's help."*

The level of brokenness described above will provide some insight into the participants' ability to do preliminary community exegesis. The ability to go to a corner or a particular location and quickly inquire with those who might be waiting on the corner for the bus or touch base with a store owner. This shows their ability, although in a fledgling form, to assess a context against what they understand about the proclamation and demonstration of good news.

Connecting with Business Owners

A key element in reaching a community, for the purpose of transformation, is to target key parts of the community. This would include reaching business owners. It would be preferred if teams stationed around locations where businesses are located. Getting connected to these business owners could be a critical first step in the process of establishing a bridge for gospel sharing and relationship building.

A biblical model for missional engagement with business owners is found in Acts 16 where the Apostle Paul was traveling with companions and interacted with Lydia, a dealer in purple accessories in Philippi (Acts 16:14-15). She is described by Luke as "a worshiper of God," which suggests that she was a religious entrepreneur, but not yet a follower of Jesus Christ. Paul and his companions reached her with the gospel. There are other instances of business owners becoming followers of Jesus specifically within the Gospels. The record of Jesus interacting with Peter, Matthew, and Zacchaeus, who were all professionals approached at their place of employment, suggests that the believer should not shy away from these critical spaces. The selected locations and the businesses provided an on-ramp for gospel witness.

We suggest that team members introduce themselves to business owners early on. The introductions should take place early during the first week of fieldwork. For example, station a group at a McDonald's restaurant. This group's goal would be to introduce themselves to the manager and hopefully the owner. They would also make purchases and even offer to purchase food for customers as an act of generous hospitality.

The opportunity to connect to business owners cannot be seen as a nuisance or afterthought. The myriad of opportunities available to serve is real and will ultimately enhance the quality of life within the community. Consider the act of cleaning up a small business parking lot and then patronizing that same establishment on a weekly basis. There's bound to be a connection established and the teams and church community should be ready to serve. A potential benefit of befriending business owners is creating Christian ambassadors in your context that are frequented by the community.

The presence of teams within the field making connections with business owners goes a long way to address any concerns store owners may have. Teams should think of business locations where foot traffic is sure to be present. Business locations like coffee shops and laundromats will always have patrons waiting for service and there are always quick opportunities to show hospitality. It is important to request permission before posting up inside of any business location. There are less obvious and illegal business locations within a neighborhood that make for great opportunities for gospel engagement. Consider corners where there is known drug dealing and/or prostitution. The weekly presence of a team, armed with resources to help, presents a redemptive path forward. While we encourage engaging certain locations, we do want to stress the need to have a blend of male presence within teams. We also recognize the importance of having someone on the team with the ability to deescalate a situation that could rapidly escalate.

Community Exegesis

The process of missional engagement requires a certain level of exegesis. Exegesis is defined as a critical explanation or interpretation of a text, especially of Scripture. The term is also useful for determining the beliefs, values and history of a community. You are finding out what makes a community tick, bringing it to the surface and using it as a tool to strategically preach and practice the gospel.

On a macro-level there is an opportunity to utilize tools such as census data and other demographic tools. There are databases that provide income, marital status, education and other things that will be critical to getting a big picture for a place. We have found that police reports are an excellent tool for forecasting needs within a community. The temptation to simply gather information for reporting can be a distraction, but it is important to connect the dots. Another option is to visit a local council person's office, obtain info and introduce yourself so that you can establish a relational bridge.

On a micro-level it is critically important to begin developing a neighborhood narrative. This is accomplished by finding the "person of peace" within the community or what one might call the town crier. This is the person that knows everything—they have dates, times and names all in their possession. In order to obtain this kind of intelligence foot soldiers are needed. This is an opportunity to involve folks who are on the sidelines.

As teams fan out into the community, they are able to obtain prominent cross streets, third places, nodes, traffic paths, districts, edges and landmarks. Two great resources that can help with this discovery exercise are *Tradecraft For the Church on Mission*[13] and *Neighborhood Mapping; How To Make Your Church Invaluable to the Community*.[14] These will be helpful tools for a church of any size looking to actively engage their surroundings.

The reality is that we never stop learning our context. The need to exhaust these contacts is realized in a pre-assessment survey designed to gauge missional engagement. There are some really good ones out there. In my past role as a missional consultant within Philadelphia and the state of Pennsylvania, there were surveys used to help churches discover their context. Within the work of community exegesis, we use a rubric to help interpret results for pastors and leaders looking to engage communities. Churches are placed on a missional continuum, which then becomes a baseline to measure missional maturation. Although we did not provide an exegesis tool within the appendix, you can find tools in the two previous works mentioned.

---

[13] Crider, C., McCrary, L., Calfee, R., & Stephens, W. (2013). *Tradecraft: For the church on mission.* Portland, OR: Urban Loft.

[14] Fuder, J. (2014). *Neighborhood mapping: How to make your church invaluable to the community.* Chicago: Moody.

Conclusion

It is incredibly important to take your time explaining and using these tools in your congregation. For many congregants these are advanced tools but they don't have to be barriers to obtain the information that can be used to do kingdom work. There is no way to insert the full package of tools that many missiologists use to reach unreached communities but these can begin building a foundation for understanding where God has sent you to serve.

The documented responses you receive will be important because you will learn from others and their reflections on victories and failures. Jesus Himself sent out the 72 disciples and ultimately received reports of their time in towns and places he planned to visit. (Luke 10:1-18)

Questions/Assignment

1. As you set out to get involved in the community phase of ministry, what do you believe will be the biggest church or organizational hurdle that needs to be overcome?

2. When you observe how Great Commission Church executed the T4T strategy, how might your fellowship differ?

3. Can you state three unique characteristics of your context?

4. Please name three community businesses that your church can bless within the next month.

5. The spiritual and missional formation phase of the training is set to help participants understand what it means to be the sent people of God wherever they find themselves. What spiritual disciplines outlined in this chapter have you picked up?

CHAPTER 5

From Outreach To Outcomes

Training for the Trenches Results

The result of three years of engaging the community through Training for the Trenches is summarized in this chapter. We believe that it is extremely beneficial to read about the ebb and flow of teams heading into the field. Our intent is to encourage you with these results so that you don't feel alone. It is always important to debrief on the happenings over each project year. As pastors and leaders we get to coach individuals through their struggles and determine ways to help others mature in their ability to reach others. We were both encouraged and shocked at some of the achievements the teams shared in their weekly updates. What you will read in this chapter are some accounts of real-life ministry struggles and successes faced by teams passionate about reaching their neighborhood.

Measuring Group Dynamics: Church

In an effort to gauge strengths and weaknesses of teams it will be helpful to use something like a questionnaire. We used something called, Group Dynamics Survey (APPENDIX D). These surveys were given to team members to gather information prior to heading into the field. Our observation was that teams weren't too high or too low; confidence was average. We realized there was going to be some growth and there was also going to be some frustration. Plain and simple, this is church life—a series of mountaintops, some mundane experiences, and then some losses. We needed to develop a culture, which conveyed the idea that every member is a missionary. The key for us was that these teams occupy the role of advocate for this training program within the broader fellowship. We also wanted to create an atmosphere where there was room to be creative within the teams.

The success of the group dynamics were important to us as we were committed to individuals working within teams to achieve stated goals. It was more important to work together than alone in both the class and field. We would suggest that anyone implementing this strategy not ignore this dynamic as we were not simply after individuals going out alone into the neighborhood but instead we wanted to deploy trained teams committed to gospel engagement. The information gathered from conversations out in the field is our bread and butter, and we must take seriously our ability to connect for three months in the field.

The challenge of working within a team and moving together toward a common goal can be a major hurdle. Consider the prospect of sharing the gospel message within a community and maintaining healthy team dynamics. The challenges are real. We encourage teams to share their experiences publicly because it will serve as an encouragement to the rest of the congregation. Sharing about struggles can spark further missional activity.

Measuring Field Conversations: Community

We developed a Conversation Survey (APPENDIX E) designed to gather week-to-week interactions between team members and the public. Much of the interaction at these particular locations would be very public and with no previously established relationship. The months of June, July, and August were the set times for the fieldwork or outdoor portion of this project. Each week the teams would meet at their designated location wearing their "Ask Me Why I'm Not in Church" T-shirts ready to engage individuals. They would have a team leader and a scribe who would record pertinent information surrounding the team's interaction.

In a nutshell the execution phase of the Training for the Trenches summer project consisted of teams showing up at locations on the first Sunday in June or the beginning of the summer months. Participants wore their "Ask Me Why I'm Not in Church" T-shirts. In some cases, teams came prepared with church business cards and some kind of tool, like the *Three Circles* booklet. The team leaders and scribes took with them pad and pen, and were asked to record the names and the phone number and/or email of contacts. The teams that set up in specific locations where businesses were prominent were asked to come prepared with cash in hand to patronize those businesses.

A key piece of this particular part of the project included participants completing the aforementioned, Conversation Survey. The groups were asked weekly to complete the online Conversation Survey—it was also stressed with the team leaders that it should be completed to communicate significant interactions with individuals at the community locations. As you venture into community you will want to capture the input of the individuals that teams are engaging.

At times many of these interactions were based on little conversation, but they left impressions on T4T team members. For us this suggested that these interactions went beyond simple introductions and seemed to initiate the beginnings of a relational bridge for Gospel witness. We also ascertained that there was an openness on behalf of the public to have someone follow-up with them. This was encouraging, and we strongly suggested that the person following up with that contact should be the person who had the initial engagement.

The subject of follow-up meant going further and exploring a deeper spiritual connection. Our hope was that groups would capture meaningful information and gauge how receptive the individual was to continuing on with a conversation about life and the Gospel. If there was an opening, which there were many, how would T4T team members follow-up with these individuals? There were several ways that they followed-up on receptive conversations. They made phone calls, sent text messages and even set up appointments to meet with individuals. We encouraged them to take ownership of establishing the bridge. We would encourage that women follow up with women and men follow up with men.

As you implement a strategy in your context you must be willing to check in and make adjustments when necessary by calling the teams in from the field, dialogue about their experiences and give further instructions prior to deploying them back to the field. There is a danger in fieldwork becoming routine or discouraging without incremental feedback from fresh eyes.

Follow Up Strategy

The follow-up response most utilized was inviting someone to attend a church worship service that Sunday or the next Sunday. There were also the invitations extended to attend small group fellowships during the week. Many Training for the Trenches team members simply stated they would, "Follow-up with the individual the following week." This is where the benefit of having a weekly presence throughout the summer is invaluable. We encourage team members to carry a list of ministries that serve the community with them and to be prepared to speak to individuals about ministries that would directly serve them, for example, Teenage Moms, Returning Citizens, Grief Counseling, etc. These other non-Sunday ministries are simply ways that Great Commission Church engages in contextual ministry.

We want to encourage you to have a real follow-up strategy. Emphasize simple steps, things like making a phone call or sending a text to individuals that a team member met out in the field. The missionality of providing a promise of direct connection to a stranger fits with the incarnational/missional culture that you are trying to establish.

Please be sure to encourage your teams to dialogue about what they believe is the best option to follow up on those that they've made initial contact with. This process is really the bread and butter of outreach and it's so often forgotten and/or neglected. This is where the tedious process of checking in week to week on the status of follow-up will become a mundane but a necessary task. The goal is to connect them to both God and fellowship within His body, the church.

Training for The Trenches Team Presentations

These presentations will be the culmination of the fieldwork over the summer months. Our teams were encouraged to be creative as they painted a picture of their engagement in the field. You should provide a mock presentation that would be a model for teams as they prepare to present their findings. The teams were given two weeks following the final Sunday in the field before team presentations would begin. The presentations were given in front of the entire church, which was useful to infuse the idea that every member was a missionary. Our desire was to drill this down to the DNA level of our fellowship.

Implementing this aspect of the Training for the Trenches project into your Sunday morning worship experience may be extreme, but putting missions in a more prominent spotlight may galvanize congregants. Consider missions to be more than an add-on or an every 5th Sunday experience. Providing space so that teams can organize and gather thoughts and experiences to display in front of others is important and a constant reminder of our local communities and our efforts to touch these communities.

Encountering the Community: Measuring Engagement

One of the key locations over the past three years of this project has been a McDonald's restaurant about a quarter of a mile from the church. This location doubles as a gas station and convenience store. At this location folks in the neighborhood can purchase a burger, a $1.00 cigarette, as well as condoms all in one location. One of the more seasoned members of our crew shared about being able to engage a number of individuals and experienced the full continuum of interactions. Her self-documentation highlights what we were looking for. She described rejection after rejection as par for the course but her persistence and creativity was out of this world. Her public testimony as well as her weekly reports embodied exactly what we were looking for in a T4T team member. The misnomer is that one conversation equals one conversion and this is a sequence that rarely shows up in Scripture or our personal lives.

The conversations between T4T team members and the community were pivotal in the overall process of facilitating community transformation. If the Gospel message is able to transform lives, then it must also transform communities. Continual engagement between the church and its neighbors will bring about the shalom of creation, which includes the transformation of broken places into restored communities.

We determined that we needed to create categories to classify our community engagement. Please reference APPENDIX F for those categories. Of the hundreds of documented interactions gathered over three years of Training for the Trenches program and fieldwork, we determined that the majority of interactions were *Seeds Planted and Watered*. Most of what was reported back week-by-week were conversations that either led to presentations of the Gospel, follow-up opportunities, or dead-end experiences.

Earlier on we briefly touched on follow-up within the T4T environment. There were a number of the interactions filed under *Seeds Planted and Watered* that ended with prayer and an invitation to church for worship or even to a small group meeting. There were a number of *Service Opportunity* for teams. The transient nature of certain locations required creativity and persistence when it came to the "how to serve." The teams with stationary locations, such as the laundromat, were able to have more *Seeds Planted and Watered* conversations. In fact, those teams reported more conversations with individuals from other faiths.

The presence of *Seeds Planted and Watered* interactions with individuals from other faiths brought to light the importance of the apologetics training provided during the T4T training. These were highly effective conversations. There were several other conversations that dipped into community politics and T4T team members were able to engage on that level, which included dispelling the negative impression that many had of the church. Reps brought back various tales of political conspiracy theories coupled with church scandals. The trope regarding churches within the community was one of irrelevance. This was a charge that resonated throughout all T4T locations.

Training for the Trenches teams were able to seize the opportunity to bless the businesses in their location by engaging in meaningful *Service Opportunity*. There were the many opportunities to clean business parking lots, hand out bottles of water, patronize businesses and bring laundry supplies and quarters just to be a blessing to the community. Over the three years of Training for the Trenches there have been a number of *Salvation Experiences*. We also had a number of individuals travel to the church on Sundays to worship with us.

Additionally, over the history of the T4T project there were community persons who met the *Discipleship within Community* designation and have become part of GCC life. The planting and watering of gospel seed eventually produced individuals who became thriving, growing believers. A unique way of understanding the above results is to consider the T4T project against the backdrop of a spiritual birth line. Stephen Smallman authored, *Spiritual Birthline: Understanding How We Experience the New Birth*.[15] In his work, he postulates that Christians must understand more fully the work of the Holy Spirit within soteriology. As understood by this researcher the work of the Holy Spirit begins long before a conversion event. Smallman says: "The beginning of the growth process is not conversion as we have seen." In his book he presents his timeline, as seen below, and it helps to reorient what the church understands about the process of salvation. In the illustration below he juxtaposes physical birth with spiritual birth.

---

[15] Smallman, S. E., & Colson, C. (2006). *Spiritual Birthline: Understanding How We Experience the New Birth*. Wheaton: Crossway Books. 25

Table 2
Spiritual Birthline

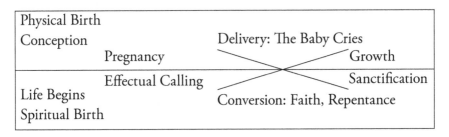

The diagram is helpful for this particular discussion because it conveys to those co-laboring in the work of the Gospel that whether they are involved in the spiritual birth or delivery process, their labor is not in vain. Smallman makes the following point: "My core perspective in all this is quite simple. I have come to believe that how we conceive of conversion determines how we do evangelism."[16] In chapter twelve of his book, the evangelizing believer is viewed as a kind of "Spiritual Midwife." This discussion gives some unique insight into the process of discipleship within the framework of evangelism. Smallman says: "We need to view discipleship as our part of what the Spirit is doing in people's lives, including the time before conversion."[17]

The work of planting and watering is significant as the followers of Christ work under the guidance and power of the Holy Spirit in the work of redemption. T4T Reps who engage their community encounter opportunities to either plant the seed of the Gospel or water that seed. Smallman identifies this as the part of the journey where someone makes noise during his or her spiritual birth.[18] We noticed that sometimes discouragement accompanied the ministry of planting and watering because of the lack of individuals actually trusting Jesus and becoming disciples of Christ. We recognize the importance of valuing the role we play in the process but also helping everyone to recognize that God is the One that gives the increase.

---

[16] Ibid.,

[17] Ibid.,

[18] Ibid.,

Two important questions to ask as leaders roll out the Training for the Trenches project are: 1) Did the T4T project facilitate the dispersion of the Gospel message while executing the call to train individuals to fulfill the great commission and the great commandment? 2) Were these groups engaging in incarnational ministry focused on bringing about shalom at a community level?

My advice for churches of various sizes and capacities is to establish a baseline (such as we did in APPENDIX F) to assess how you are reaching your context. Our baseline may not work for you but to not adopt a rubric for measuring results and effectiveness may be removing accountability from the process. This is a growth area for churches even though measuring our interactions may seem clinical and secular. I would encourage you to consider this aspect of the T4T project as a form of journaling that ultimately leads to rejoicing.

Questions

1. Within our results-driven culture the church sometimes equates bigger numbers with doing or heading in the right direction. How would you measure results after reading this chapter?

2. Who possesses ultimate responsibility for building the church? And why?

3. Can you identify three ways that you can be incarnational within your immediate community?

4. Please list three prayers that you can put into action that will help you and your church family engage your surroundings.

CHAPTER 6

Why Use Training For The Trenches As A Ministry Motif

Training for the Trenches is a motif of ministry birthed out of a particular context. We sought to provide a clean presentation that would be easily transferred to any context, but with a sensitivity to context. Our task here was to present one example formed within a largely urban African-American community. We wanted to present a missionally rich perspective on how incarnational ministry could develop through a church of any size. Of course this is not a magic pill that will work anywhere, but we believe that the growth of the body of Christ happens through sanctification and multiplication.

Taking the Context Seriously

There is room for further dialogue on incarnational ministry, and the following is an abbreviation and summation of the project's missiological roots. Dr. Susan Baker, an urban missiologist, provides a backdrop for understanding many of the challenges of urban incarnational ministry in the book, *The Urban Face of Mission: Ministering the Gospel in a Diverse and Changing World*. In a chapter entitled, "The Social Sciences: Tools for Urban Ministry," she provides an overview of some of the challenges of doing urban ministry. She states that missionaries who have had to serve cross culturally have had to be incarnational due to the limitations of being the foreigner in a place, but many who have a short ride into urban communities see little need for an incarnational way of fulfilling the disciple-making call.[19]

She goes on to provide a clear purpose for incarnational ministry when she said: "The main purpose of incarnational ministry is to assist us in understanding the community and its needs from the inside."[20] Her dialogue around this topic is without question helpful as there is an insistence to utilize the tools (in this case sociological tools) that are available, but to never assume that tools are a conclusion or remedy. There is a priority to know the needs of a community, or as Baker explains, churches must do a "needs assessment."[21]

Baker refers to the tools that are necessary for urban ministry. Her treatment of "contextualization" is critical to this dialogue. She provides some clarity to this concept by stating: "Contextualization presupposes that Christian theology has one foot in the biblical revelation and the other foot in the historical and cultural context of the people hearing the message."[22] We are not suggesting a dismissal of good Christian theology, but we are asking for caution as you consider to whom you are preaching good theology. She goes on to clarify her point further with: "A theology based on questions that are irrelevant to the listener will soon be discarded as useless."[23] There is no division between the work of doing good theology and the work of determining my audience and their needs.

Contextualization is a tool used by many churches to facilitate the process of reaching individuals who are well outside of the culture and community of faith. Churches that find themselves within a heterogeneous community, will find this style of ministry useful. Michael Frost and Alan Hirsch defined contextualization this way: "To contextualize is

---

[19] Conn, H. M., Ortiz, M., & Baker, S. S. (2002). *The urban face of mission: Ministering the Gospel in a diverse and changing world.* Phillipsburg, NJ: P & R Pub.
[20] Ibid., 71
[21] Ibid., 74-75
[22] Ibid., 75
[23] Ibid., 76

to understand the language, longings, lifestyle patterns, and worldview of the host community and to adjust our practices accordingly without compromising the gospel."[24] A proper understanding of contextualization helps in a dialogue centered on seeking Gospel-centered change within a cultural context.

We Must Ask Before We Assume

A significant part of incarnational ministry involves asking what the needs are, and additionally having a presence within the community. Training for the Trenches sought at some level to fulfill the idea of having presence within the community through this project. This project and its aim fit within the larger cultural proclivity of Great Commission Church as a missional church. Consider how Halter and Smay link missional and incarnational. Missional has an inseparable twin. It's called "incarnational."

> *The root meaning of Incarnation: any person or thing serving as the type of embodiment of a quality or concept. Specifically, it means to embody in the flesh. John 1:14 gives us the picture: "And the Word (Jesus) became flesh and made his dwelling among us." [KJV] The missional part was Jesus leaving his Father's side in the heavens and coming to us in the form of a human. The incarnational part was how he took on flesh and lived with us. Said another way, missional sentness is focused on leaving and everything related to going, but incarnational represents how we go and what we do as we go.[25]*

Based on Halter and Smay, incarnational ministry parallels in a unique way what it means to be missional, and it is worth considering that these

---

[24] Frost, M., & Hirsch, A. (2003). The shaping of things to come: innovation and mission for the 21st- century church. Peabody, MA: Hendrickson. 85
[25] Ibid., 38

are not interchangeable terms.[26] Contextualization seems to be more of a tool utilized within incarnational ministry. As churches learn to utilize this tool, there is the possibility of creating and reaching sojourners. Theologian David Bosch suggests, in comments regarding contextualization, that the church must understand the connection between mission and contextualization. He says:

> *The historical world situation is not merely an exterior condition for the church's mission; rather it ought to be incorporated as a constitutive element into our understanding of mission, its aim and its organization (Rutti 1972:231). Such posture is in full accord with Jesus' understanding of his mission, as reflected in our gospel; he did not soar off into heavenly heights but immersed himself into the altogether real circumstances of the poor, the captives, the blind, the oppressed (cf. Lk 4:18f). Today, too, Christ is where the hungry and the sick are, the exploited and the marginalized. The power of his resurrection propels human history toward the end, under the banner "Behold, I make all things new!" Revelation 21:5 [KJV]"*[27]

Bosch links the incarnation of Christ alongside the present ministry of the church. There is intentional linkage between Christology and missiology. God not only provides a rich picture of incarnation in the Scriptures, which prompts believers to worship, but in the person of Jesus Christ the church is also given the impetus for action (John 20:21; Romans 1:2-5). The motif for ministry undertaken by this one church is one that relies heavily on an understanding of the lead pastor's understanding of what it means to be a missional church within an urban context.

---

[26] David Fitch adds to this conversation in his book, "Faithful Presence." In regard to "mission Dei and the incarnation and the church, "Here, in this space of the church, shaped by the disciplines, the mission Dei meets the incarnation of God in the Son to produce the witness of the church." There is more work to be done to both link and distinguish them as important callings for the church of Christ. Fitch, D. E. (2016). *Faithful Presence: Seven disciplines that shape the church for mission.*200

[27] Bosch, D. J. (1991). *Transforming mission: paradigm shifts in theology of mission.* Maryknoll, NY: Orbis Books.426

In a dissertation submitted in the summer of 2010, Larry Anderson laid out the model that had been utilized to reach the West Oak Lane community. The thesis of his work, "The Missional Gospel: Ministering to A Community With the Whole Gospel Through Its Existing Social Services"[28] provided a missional/incarnational ministry foundation for the T4T project started in the summer of 2016. This particular model has guided GCC in the real world articulation of the gospel to its neighbors in West Oak Lane. Anderson imports Dr. Perkins' model as a rough template for his project. Regarding Perkins he says the following:

> *Perkins articulated why evangelism was not enough and how both white evangelicals and the black church failed to rise to the challenge of biblical justice in America. But even more importantly, Perkins came up with a strategy; a blueprint coined the Three R's of Christian Community Development— Relocation, Reconciliation, and Redistribution—to provide a holistic approach to ministry.*[29]

Larry's dissertation work is a precursor to the work within this book. He articulates a strategy to attain a robust, missionally driven, incarnationally focused contextual ministry within the city. His articulation of the missional gospel provides a motif for the kind of ministry that the T4T project sought to undertake. Anderson posits:

> *The missional church employing the missional hermeneutic develops its missional theology and practices its findings in a local context seeking to follow Christ. Taking the missional approach means assuming the position of a missionary to one's context and investigating its people, culture, habits, and relevant statistical data, while praying for God's wisdom and favor in trying to reconcile all of that to him.*[30]

---

[28] Anderson, L. L. (2010). The missional gospel: ministering to a community with the whole gospel through its existing social services. Hatfield, PA.: Biblical Theological Seminary.

[29] Ibid., 42

[30] Ibid., 37

The challenge to experiment with two dissimilar organizations in order to reach a community lays the foundation for the kind of interaction we engaged in during our time in West Oak Lane. Larry's thesis connected GCC with social service agencies within West Oak Lane to observe whether symbiotic relationships within urban communities are viable relationships.

Presence Matters More Than We Realize

Great Commission Church has put into practice the priority of connecting with its community. This fits with what we understand about being incarnational. Anderson further states, "The church must no longer settle for its little corner of society, which is being reduced daily, but instead decide to impact its community through partnerships."[31] Paul Sparks, Tim Soerens, and Dwight J. Friesen reference a concept that gives a framework for understanding shared space, such as a neighborhood. These authors propose a way of envisioning community as "new commons," which means " ...all dimensions of life for which everyone in your neighborhood shares a common concern." They propose that faithful presence within these *new commons* is a way for believing communities to engage and build healthy relationships within a community. Being among the people and having a faithful presence with the following four categories parallels what GCC has been consistently attempting to fulfill within this community in the following four categories: 1) Economy, 2) Environment, 3) Civic, and 4) Education.[32] These categories represent various sectors of communities. The ability to target these quadrants with missional intention may prove helpful for churches existing within post-Christian urban centers.

GCC Connecting with the Community

We found these categories useful to gauge our engagement of the West Oak Lane community during the fieldwork portion of the project. The

---

[31] Ibid., 101

[32] Sparks, P., Sorens, T., & Friesen, D. J. (2014). *The new parish: how neighborhood churches are transforming mission, discipleship and community*. Downers Grove, IL: InterVarsity Press. pp.95-96

events/ministries represent outreach efforts undertaken since the church's move into the West Oak Lane community in 2008.

There have been 38 corporate outreach ministry initiatives undertaken by GCC since 2008. There is a distinction that the events/ministries listed below are corporate versus individual outreach efforts because of the unique outcomes between corporate and individual evangelism at GCC. One can observe that the bulk of attention has been focused on ministering to the economic and educational disparity within this West Oak Lane community. The categories take into consideration felt-needs ministry, but it must be stated that a key commitment remains communicating the Gospel as these initiatives are being executed. We do not see a dichotomy between the preaching and the presence of the Gospel. There are parallel activities taking place; good news coupled with good deeds. We have either initiated, managed or simply observed up close that the above ministry endeavors are essential to doing kingdom work within our context.

Table 3
GCC 2008-2019 Categorized Presence in WOL

GCC Outreach Activities Since 2008					
Event Ministry	**Economy**	**Environment**	**Civic**	**Education**	**Frequency**
Hope 4 Philly	x	x	x		Annual
Vacation Bible School				x	Annual
Thanksgiving Baskets	x				Annual
Youth Basketball Outreach				x	Seasonal
Stanton Family Manor	x			x	Weekly
Simon's Rec Ctr: Renovations	x	x			Annual
Mentoring: PPE, MLK, PCAT	x		x	x	Weekly
Penny Packer Elementary	x	x	x	x	Seasonal
Black History Program			x	x	Annual
Fire Victims Emergency Crisis	x				As Needed
Chemo Care Packages	x				As Needed
Alpha Pregnancy	x			x	OneTime
Girl'sCircle				x	Weekly

Tabor Children's Shelter	x				OneTime
Recovery House (Men's House)	x			x	Weekly
Prison Ministry	x			x	Weekly
Neighborhood Block Party	x	x	x	x	Annual
Phillies Game For Community Kids				x	One Time
Community Prayer Walk	x		x		Seasonal
Gift Wrapping at Cheltenham Mall	x				Annual
Block Cleaning/Plants		x			Annual
Pop-Up Prayer Vernon Park		x	x		Seasonal
14th District Prayer Walks		x	x		Seasonal
A Few Good Men Father's Day Award		x	x	x	Seasonal
Muffins with Moms				x	Seasonal
Training for the Trenches	x	x	x		Annual
Donuts with Dads				x	Seasonal
Emergency Meals to Families	x				As Needed
Emergency Clothing Drive	x	x			As Needed
West Oak Lane Breast Cancer Walk	x			x	One Time
Walk for Autism	x		x	x	Annual
Women's Self Defense Training			x	x	One Time
Young Lives	x		x	x	Monthly
Community Forgiveness & Restoration	x		x	x	Weekly
CHAI: Trauma Workshops			x	x	Seasonal
R.U.T.H.: Redeeming Us Through Healing				x	Seasonal
Addiction Recovery Ministry			x	x	As Needed
Gone Too Soon' Grief Ministry				x	As Needed

In this chapter we observed that ministry grows out of a commitment to investigate the community and determine real needs. We've gone through the nuts and bolts of incarnational ministry and now we are ready to pull out some key principles that should guide our missional engagement. We want to encourage freshness and creativity and not blind mimicking of other mission models that do not consider context seriously.

CONCLUSION

Lessons For The Broader Church

Training for the Trenches is just a framework for other churches who are looking to engage their context. The three-part strategy consists of 1) Initiating Conversation, 2) Sunday Fieldwork and 3) Location. As outlined in Chapter 4, this strategy is designed to get churches out of the building at critical moments. The understanding that the church is the sent people of God coupled with a strategy that disrupts a traditional church setting could help many churches connect with their community (John 20:21).

An incarnational approach requires a working knowledge of contextualization and a commitment to exegete one's context. It is believed that the framework proposed could assist churches looking to make a missional turn. The opportunity to undertake a missional/incarnational study of Luke 4:14-22 should provide a biblical model for engaging varied and unique ministry settings. An example that any church should consider emulating is the processes of always asking questions of the community versus assuming to know a place and the people of the place. Another critical step is prayer, specifically for the leadership and the power of God the Holy Spirit in the work of Gospel witnessing. GCC considers the incarnation of Christ as not just the theological activity of God, but a model of how to engage the marginalized. The Apostle Paul states very clearly as he writes about the *kenosis*[33] of Jesus Christ:

In your relationships with one another, have the same mindset as Christ Jesus:

> Your attitude should be the same as that of Christ Jesus: If you have any encouragement from Who, being in very nature God, did not consider equality with God something to be grasped, but made himself nothing, taking the very nature of a servant, being made in human likeness. And being found in appearance as a man, he humbled himself and became obedient to death--even death on a cross! Phil. 2:5-8 NIV

Since the Savior humbled Himself to reach humanity, should not His church operate in similar fashion? Ross Hastings captures in this statement the ramification of the incarnational ministry: "Jesus himself, as God the Son, entered by his incarnation into a specific human context and communicated the nature of God and the Gospel in ways that were culturally relevant without ever compromising his holiness and without capitulating to sinful cultural trends."[34] If the church follows in the discipleship paradigm commanded by Christ, then the church must be diligent in replicating the ministry lessons first displayed by the Lord.

---

[33] *Kenosis* – the self-emptying of Christ. Stanley Grenz states the following regarding the kenosis theory, "Rather, the Son gave up the independent exercise of these powers. In other words, although he retained all the attributes, power, or prerogatives of God. The earthly Jesus refused to draw on his divine abilities merely at his own whim. Rather, he willingly submitted his prerogative to use his divine capabilities to his Father's will as directed by the Spirit." Grenz, S. J. (1994). *Theology for the community of God*. Nashville, TN: Broadman & Holman. 307

[34] Hastings, R. (2012). *Missional God, missional church: hope for re-evangelizing the West*. Downers Grove, IL: IVP Academic.61

Give Birth, Don't Clone

My earliest memory of cloning was in the early 1980s at a Christian movie theater just outside Philadelphia. The movie was something contrived by a popular "End Times" writer and ultimately put on the big screen for hundreds of youth groups and their leaders flocking to see this horrible B movie. Of course, there are some things that we want cloned or copied—things like recipes or photos, but there are other things that really shouldn't be copied. Take ministries or churches, we should be careful not to simply replicate something that's out there that worked in another context but may not work in your world. What looks great in the suburbs could be disastrous in the city and vice versa.

Our ministries should be Spirit-led and biblically informed, which will ensure that the right ingredients are included in the foundational phase of a ministry or a church. If we are praying and seeking God's direction, and referencing the ministry of Christ, then we are on good footing. In fact, we are being good disciples. I believe God is looking for us to give birth instead of copying something that we've seen in another person's ministry backyard. This will take patience, dedication, and a reorientation toward cultural change and replication.

Nothing about Training for the Trenches is meant to be cloned. If we are cloning, then we are not doing incarnational ministry. So we are encouraging you to be like the sons of Issachar and know the times (1 Chronicles 12:32). So much of what we see in Western Christianity is an attempt to mirror popular ministries or mega church pastors. We want to encourage you to commit to presence like our Savior who dwelled with us (John 1:14). The Spirit will lead us, and Christ will build His church (Matthew 16:18; John 16:13).

Our encouragement would be to please be authentic and original. Do the work of community exegesis, ask good questions, introduce yourself, and be known in your context. Most importantly, pray to the Lord of the harvest as you are about His work. We have presented a case study based on our experience in a community with tons of needs. A big part of how we arrived in West Oak Lane and began Training for the Trenches is tied to our commitment to never hold something so tight that it becomes repetitious instead Spirit-led. I believe that when we serve our communities well we take part in introducing heaven on earth.

Appendix A

Sample Half Day Prayer Guide

The following statements and Scriptures are a suggested guide for the Half Day Prayer for the Community.

Pray to see people as Jesus saw them. Matthew 9:36

Pray to recognize the idols in their lives and have the courage to speak to it. Acts 17:16-34

Pray for willing workers. Luke 10:1-2

Pray to understand the times and culture of the community and have the ability to speak to it. 1 Chronicles 12:32

Pray for resources in order to repair community breaches. Nehemiah
1:4-11

Pray for a heart that is able to engage and embrace the unsaved. Matthew
9:10

Appendix B

T4T Representative Survey

T4T Representative Survey
(Name: _____)

Team Name: _____

Please answer all questions. Your responses are confidential

How would you rate your level of confidence prior to going out to your community location?

o   I am extremely fearful and would be OK not going
o   I am committed to go but I expect to be embarrassed by my lack of knowledge
o   I want to hit the corners but I'm still concerned about my effectiveness
o   I am looking forward to hitting these corners and I am moderately confident
o   I am very confident about going to my T4T location

How would you rate your experience doing relational evangelism?

o   I have no experience doing relational evangelism
o   I have very little experience (only once in my life)
o   I have some experience doing relational evangelism (more than once in my life)

o   I am experienced doing relational evangelism (frequent communication with people on the street about Jesus)

o   I would consider myself a seasoned individual who regularly hits the streets to connect with them about new life in Christ.

Could you provide your personal barriers to fully participating in the T4T summer engagement?

Share how you believe the gospel should touch individuals?

APPENDIX C

Community Location Survey

(Name: _____)

Team Name: _____

How and why did you pick the location where you will be during July and August?

Please describe the outward/visible signs of brokenness that you see in your location.

As you talked with individuals in the community, what are the themes of brokenness that arise out of conversations, e.g., familial, marital, communal, etc?

How many individuals have you touched on this T4T trip into the community?

Why do you believe that this location provided the maximum contact possible on a Sunday morning?

Appendix D

Group Dynamics Survey

Please complete the T4T survey as frankly as possible. (Your responses are confidential.)

Your Name: _____

Team Name: _____

How would you rate your team when it comes to teamwork?

- o Poor (We do not work well together. There are other agendas.)
- o Concerned about how we will work together.
- o Average (There is some fearfulness and lack of confidence, but we are willing to go.)
- o Good (We work together well indoors, but wondering about the unknown.)
- o Excellent (We are a model for how a team should operate.)

What is your greatest strength as a team prior to going out for the first time?

What is your greatest weakness as a team prior to going out for the first time?

What do you believe you personally bring to this team?

Are you confident that all of your team is prayerful and taking this seriously?

APPENDIX E

Conversation Survey

Please complete the T4T survey as frankly as possible. (Your responses are confidential.)

If you were able to obtain the name and contact information for the person you connected with today please include their information (e.g., phone number, email, address, etc.) **Do not include your name**

Based on your conversation with this individual, how would you rate them on this spiritual continuum?

o   No spiritual awareness or concern for God
o   They have some spiritual awareness but it's all a form of godliness
o   They are searching for answers and willing to listen but …
o   They have an openness to discuss God, but still searching
o   They are very much ready to become a follower of Jesus

As you left the conversation, was there a real opening for following up with this individual?

If there was an opening, what is your follow-up strategy?

How did you prepare to answer the questions related to the T-shirt that you wore at your designated locations?

Your name please: _____

Appendix F

Measuring Community Engagement

We believed it was important to measure how Great Commission Church measured community engagement. To measure the level of interactions, we used the following list of categories:

Seed Planted/Watered (SPW) – This was selected to identify both an initial communication of the gospel message out in the field as well as a follow-up event. A watering event may be an invitation to church or a phone call, text or a conversation that was meant to lead an unbeliever to faith in Christ (1 Corinthians 3:6-7).

Service Opportunity (SO) – This is an event where T4T participants were able to engage in an act of hospitality, environmental stewardship, public prayer, or a kind act for a denizen, business, or resident.

Salvation Experience (SE) – If a T4T participant led someone to Christ as a result of contact during the designated times of the project.

Discipleship within Community (DC) – Did someone come to faith in Christ and then joined Great Commission Church and is currently being discipled?

BIBLIOGRAPHY

(2011, April 23). Rob Bell - " Bullhorn Guy " Nooma Response. Retrieved January 16, 2017, from http://www.youtube.com/watch?v=M2WopYbO9rQ

3 Circles: Life Conversation Guide | Life on Mission. (n.d.). Retrieved November 30, 2016, from http://lifeonmissionbook.com/conversation-guide

Anderson, L. L. (2010). *The missional gospel: ministering to a community with the whole gospel through its existing social services.* Hatfield, PA.: Biblical Theological Seminary.

Bosch, D. J. (1991). *Transforming mission: paradigm shifts in theology of mission.* Maryknoll, NY: Orbis Books

Brown, J. (n.d.). How we cut youth violence in Boston by 79 percent. Retrieved January 16, 2017, from http://www.ted.com/talks/jeffrey_brown_how_we_cut_youth_violence_in_boston_by_79_percent

Canty, D. K. (2017). *Developing and implementing a strategy for gospel-centered social change within the West Oak Lane community.* Hatfield, PA.: Biblical Theological Seminary.

Conn, H. M., Ortiz, M., & Baker, S. S. (2002). *The urban face of mission: Ministering the Gospel in a diverse and changing world.* Phillipsburg, NJ: P & R Pub.

Crider, C., McCrary, L., Calfee, R., & Stephens, W. (2013). *Tradecraft: For the church on mission.* Portland, OR: Urban Loft.

Elliff, T. (N.D.). *Unwanted Gift; Hearing God In The Midst Of Your Struggles.*: CLC Publications.

Fitch, D. E. (2016). *Faithful Presence: Seven disciplines that shape the church for mission.*

Franke, J. R. (2005). *The character of theology: An introduction to its nature, task, and purpose.* Grand Rapids, MI: Baker Academic.

Frost, M., & Hirsch, A. (2003). *The shaping of things to come: innovation and mission for the 21ˢᵗ- century church.* Peabody, MA: Hendrickson.

Fuder, J., & Runyon (2014). *Neighborhood mapping: How to make your church invaluable to the community.* Chicago: Moody.

Grenz, S. J. (1994). *Theology for the community of God.* Nashville, TN: Broadman & Holman.

Halter, H., & Smay, M. (2008). *The tangible kingdom: creating incarnational community: the posture and practices of ancient church now.* San Francisco, CA: Jossey-Bass.

Hastings, R. (2012). *Missional God, missional church: hope for re-evangelizing the West.* Downers Grove, IL: IVP Academic.

Ingram, C. (2007). *Good to great in God's eyes: 10 practices great Christians have in common.* Grand Rapids: Baker Books.

Leary, J. D. (2017). *Post traumatic slave syndrome: Americas legacy of enduring injury and healing.* Portland, OR: Joy DeGruy Publications. Doi

McNeal, R. (2009). *Missional renaissance: changing the scorecard for the church.* San Francisco, CA: Jossey-Bass.

Smallman, S. E., & Colson, C. (2006). *Spiritual Birthline: Understanding How We Experience the New Birth*. Wheaton: Crossway Books.

Sparks, P., Soerens, T., & Friesen, D. J. (2014). *The new parish: how neighborhood churches are transforming mission, discipleship and community*. Downers Grove, IL: InterVarsity Press.

Spiritual Gifts | FREE Spiritual Gifts Survey | Assessment, Analysis, Test. (n.d.). Retrieved May 30, 2019, from https://gifts.churchgrowth.org/spiritual-gifts-survey/

Wright, C. J. (2010). *The mission of God's people: A biblical theology of the churches mission*. Grand Rapids, MI: Zondervan.

CPSIA information can be obtained
at www.ICGtesting.com
Printed in the USA
BVHW030801040819
555043BV00001B/129/P

9 781973 664710